T0316776

ECONOMIC PROBLEMS

OF

PEACE AFTER WAR

CAMBRIDGE
UNIVERSITY PRESS

32 Avenue of the Americas, New York NY 10013-2473, USA

Cambridge University Press is part of the University of Cambridge.

It furthers the University's mission by disseminating knowledge in the pursuit of
education, learning and research at the highest international levels of excellence.

www.cambridge.org
Information on this title: www.cambridge.org/9781107433151

© Cambridge University Press 1917

This publication is in copyright. Subject to statutory exception
and to the provisions of relevant collective licensing agreements,
no reproduction of any part may take place without the written
permission of Cambridge University Press.

First published 1917
First paperback edition 2014

A catalogue record for this publication is available from the British Library

ISBN 978-1-107-43315-1 Paperback

Cambridge University Press has no responsibility for the persistence or accuracy of
URLs for external or third-party internet websites referred to in this publication,
and does not guarantee that any content on such websites is, or will remain, accurate
or appropriate.

ECONOMIC PROBLEMS

OF

PEACE AFTER WAR

THE W. STANLEY JEVONS LECTURES AT
UNIVERSITY COLLEGE, LONDON, IN 1917

BY

WILLIAM ROBERT SCOTT

M.A., D.Phil., Litt.D., LL.D.

Adam Smith Professor of Political Economy in the University of Glasgow
and Fellow of the British Academy

Cambridge:
at the University Press
1917

As Demosthenes, with often breathing up the hill,
amended his stammering; so we hope, with sundry
labours against the air, to correct our studies.

LYLY, *Campaspe.*

FOREWORD

NO doubt there will be an increasing number of those persons, who develop great wisdom after the event, who will tell us not only that they expected a great European war in which Germany would be opposed to us but that they predicted the outbreak in the summer of 1914. There may be a great satisfaction in *paulo-post-futurum* vaticinations, but the majority of us will be candid enough to admit that hostilities were unexpected, and the outbreak found the nation very gravely unprepared. It would be wise that peace should not find us unready for it; and the following pages constitute an attempt to state some of the problems which will then confront us.

Warmly as the coming of a satisfying peace will be welcomed, it must be admitted that it is difficult to picture the social and industrial conditions which must then be dealt with. "War," as Burke said, "never leaves where it found a nation." Very many phenomena will be greatly changed, and the framing of detailed forecasts is likely to result in disappointment. But it seems possible that something may be accomplished in applying general principles based upon the teaching of Economics or on the experience of somewhat similar conditions in the past, or, again, upon known dispositions of human nature. Conclusions of this character will not, and cannot, predict details, but they may present an outline of the general appearance which economic life may assume, and it will be at least of some value to have an indication of the course which progress may be expected to take, even though we cannot tell all the particular diversions that may be encountered.

When the enquiry is stated in this way, there is a difficulty at the start. In so far as reliance must be placed upon previous economic analysis, how far does it apply during a state of war? Is a study of the Economics of War a possibility? If so, what is to be said of patriotism, and is it possible that the two ideas should be reconciled or is any reconciliation required?

The making of arrangements of several kinds "for the duration of the war," suggests the conception of the period of hostilities as a species of economic *dies non*, and one wonders if this view is valid. Again, there is the restriction of individual freedom both by military service and by very many emergency measures, and the problem suggests itself as to what will be the relation of the State to economic activities after the war. Will vested interests in State-control of industry survive the war?

Then, as a special branch of these questions, there will be the position of overseas trade—will it be missionary or militant? The prominence of the submarine and likewise of air-craft may exert an influence upon the communications of Greater Britain. Defence may assume new forms, and will it be that the joint-effect of the embers of national animosity and the frustrating of the so-called German peaceful penetration may introduce a new arrangement of trade within Greater Britain and with Allied nations?

Whether we will or no, forecasts of the future must be framed. But hitherto this has been attempted in detail and purely empirically. Is it not possible to formulate the chief conditions which affect the faculty for anticipating the future, so as to have some means of correcting errors which may be expected to arise from the abnormal circumstances? For instance, may not the possible optimism of the first months of peace involve some risk of a crisis; or again, if that be avoided, may not there be a later danger-point when revived commerce and industry might be pulled up sharply by a scarcity of capital?

Some light on the last question may be obtained from consideration of the psychological basis of saving. This, together with the chances of war, has revolutionised many standards of living. Such standards, again, are largely influenced by habit, and this suggests the further problem whether it may possibly happen that standards of life may be constituted on a proportionately lower scale, leaving a larger margin for peace-time savings than in the past.

Finally, what is to be the future arrangement of industry? "Organisation" seems to have become a term which is supposed to supply an answer; but that can scarcely be, when it is commonly used in different meanings. Is it possible that the influence of Evolutionary theory may have disguised the fundamental facts? May it not be that what has been considered a process is in reality a problem—namely how to unite in any act of Production the various factors (both human and inanimate) with the least resistance? Will there be State-intervention in this, and will it help or hinder? Should it take place, would it impair initiative?

These problems have many affinities, and they meet and interlace at many points. This fact, as well as the form of lectures into which the attempted solutions have been cast, will explain the reasons why the same topic is treated in different places—usually because the aspect is somewhat different from that previously discussed. But when the word "solutions" is used, it is not to be understood in the sense of a promise to solve these and other problems which have presented themselves. It is easy to dogmatise about the future; it is difficult to trace continuity when there has been a great upheaval such as that at present. Between the present time and the period at which the economic life will have become normal again, some, and it may be many, causes will come into action, the existence of which at present can be little more than guessed at. In such cases prediction may show more boldness than discretion. But that does not mean that the attempt to provide for the future is to be abandoned as a hopeless labour. Rather something may be accomplished, if, as a result of careful analysis, a way is discovered of re-stating a troublesome problem in a form that makes it more manageable. This, it is true, is not a solution, but it may be a very considerable step forward towards the solution.

W. R. S.

April, 1917.

CONTENTS

III. COMMUNICATIONS OF A MARITIME STATE.

IV. THE SURPRISES OF PEACE.

V. SAVING AND THE STANDARD OF LIFE.

VI. ORGANISATION RE-ORIENTATED.

APPENDIX.—STATISTICS OF SHIPPING DURING WAR.

THE ECONOMIC MAN AND
A WORLD AT WAR

He was a man
Versed in the world as pilot in his compass.
The needle pointed ever to that interest
Which was his lodestar.

The Deceiver, A Tragedy.

Noble princes and knights, it is known throughout the world how ye, abandoning those delights which ye might have possessed in your hands, have chosen rather to follow the honourable profession of arms, and encounter all dangers to gain the praise of prowess and redress wrongs,....this indeed is to your fair renown and to the service of Almighty God, for in this have ye done that for which ye were born, succoring the oppressed and beating down the evil-doers. But in this, what should most elate us is the defiance which we have thus given to two so high and powerful princes as are the Emperor of Rome and King Lisuarte, with whom, if they will not be brought to reason and justice, we must perforce have great debate and warfare. Noble sirs, what then have we to expect? Certes nothing but that defending the right and reasonable cause against those who would support injustice, we shall gain yet more victories, such that the whole world shall ring therewith.

Amadis of Gaul (Southey's Version).

THE ECONOMIC MAN AND
A WORLD AT WAR

Ministers in Parliament and writers in the Press have often, since the outbreak of war, alluded to the violation of economic principles, assuming that this has been one of the consequences of the existence of a state of hostilities. The Latin maxim *inter arma leges silent* is applied to the suspension or abrogation of what was known formerly as economic law. But it may be guessed that there is involved here some confusion of ideas which are essentially different in their nature. In so far as Political Economy makes any claim to be considered to be a science, it is difficult to conceive it as one of an intermittent character, the conclusions of which only apply in time of peace. Indeed, if that were so, what are we to say of the whole former subject-matter of the study during a period of hostilities? Has it disappeared, or has it so changed its form that it has been subsumed under some subordinate part of the military art? After the long years of peace which this country has enjoyed, it adds to the chaos if we must think of economic activity as anarchical, or as existing only on sufferance threatened by a sword of Damocles suspended over it. The Defence of the Realm Act and the almost innumerable administrative measures which have resulted from it, show that both the extent and the manner of commercial and industrial activity have undergone great changes since the summer of 1914, and in the making of these changes principles, which were formerly accepted, have been avowedly disregarded.

When this situation is considered, a half-formed impression begins to emerge, namely that there is no little difference of opinion as to what is the nature of economic investigation and

its teaching.   If we evoke from the past that enigmatic spirit
—"the economic man"—he would no doubt have much to say
of the present situation.   If he be conceived solely as "a being
who desires to possess wealth and as capable of judging of the
comparative efficacy of means for obtaining that end," and if
abstraction be made "of every other passion or motive except
those which may be regarded as perpetually antagonising principles[1]," then the spirit in which wealth and larger things than
wealth are being sacrificed must appear strange and anomalous.
But "the economic man" proved the Delphic oracle of the
nineteenth century whose sayings masked under a clear-cut
precision many practical ambiguities.   His personality, under
the guise of an abstract simplicity, concealed almost baffling
complexities.   Nor has he been happy in some of his commen-
tators, so that one is inclined to exclaim with Dangle in *The
Critic*, "Egad, I think the interpreter is the harder to be understood of the two."   It is needless to repeat the sneers of Carlyle
and Ruskin against a series of conceptions which the latter
held to be "absolutely incompetent or absolutely false[2]," but
the existence of a discrepancy in the point of view may be
illustrated by two opposed quotations from two works which
bear the same title—*Wealth and Welfare*—and, by an even
greater coincidence, from pages numbered alike in each of the
two books.   The earlier volume was written by Commander
Hastings Berkley and was printed in 1887.   He declares that
"from the orthodox school there grows up in logical sequence, a
system of Political Economy, which, but for the good sense and
good feeling of the generality of men, would issue in the most
revolting applications[3]."   The second *Wealth and Welfare* is
the well-known treatise of Professor Pigou in which it is stated
that "the purpose of economic investigation is not primarily
scientific, if by science we understand the single-eyed search
after knowledge for its own sake, it is rather practical and

---

[1] Mill, *Essays on Some Unsettled Principles of Political Economy*, 1844,
p. 137.

[2] Ruskin, *Munera Pulveris*, 1886, p. xviii; *Time and Tide by Wear
and Tyne*, 1872, pp. 176, 177.

[3] p. 4.

utilitarian[1]." Certainly it would be a most jaundiced critic who would apply the epithet "revolting" to the broad humanity of the later book, and this shows us that there is a misconception which requires to be discussed, and, as a result of the discussion, perhaps removed.

In order to secure a firm foundation for the treatment of Economics and War, it is necessary first to clear up the conception of the "economic man" in this connection. Those who formed the celebrated abstraction were perfectly clear in their own minds that the abstract conception was no more than a starting-point. Thus J. S. Mill, while for purposes of study he concentrates attention upon the desire of Wealth, points out at the same time that social phenomena are interdependent and that "there is, perhaps, no action of a man's life in which he is neither under the immediate nor the remote influence of any impulse but the desire of wealth[2]." The other desires were treated, or to be treated, in separate branches of Social Science; and it was only when the results of these had been brought into relation with those provided by Political Economy that the "economic man" emerged from his isolated abstractedness and became a real human being. Much of the misconception has been due to the impatience with which some readers accepted the *homo economicus* as an actual typical British citizen, thus neglecting the synthesis which is clearly conditioned by the previous abstraction. Accordingly, to charge the "economic man" with a neglect of morals is as much out of place as to blame a theory of chess with failing to take account of the art of cooking[3]! Or in other words we are in fact trying to treat pure Economics as if they were both Applied and Social Economics[4].

It has been claimed for the "economic man" that "he was not selfish[5]," and he was certainly not a pacifist. Ricardo explicitly takes account of and approves a war which involved

[1] p. 4.   [2] J. S. Mill, *System of Logic*, II. pp. 494–8.
[3] Pareto, *Manuel d'Économie Politique*, Paris, 1909, I. p. 18.
[4] Walras, *Éléments d'Économie Politique Pure*, 1874, pp. 32, 33.
[5] Marshall, *Present Position of Economics*, 1885, p. 28.

some "great national interest[1]," and Professor Edgeworth, when dealing with a similar abstraction, expressly states that the fundamental principle works under two aspects—the one being a state of war and the other one of contract[2].

Thus it follows that, even the severe and rigid conception of the "economic man" does not exclude his entering voluntarily into a state of war when his interests require it; or it may perhaps be added, when those interests which he included in his own, or regarded as his own, demanded it. But the modern economist has supplemented the conception of the "economic man" by an explicit declaration of his relationship to the community of which he is a citizen, and this development has brought more nearly within the range of economics a definite recognition of social relationships. That attitude makes the participation of the man of affairs in a necessary war more clear and not far from inevitable. A wide view of the citizen's real interest may show him that his continued free enjoyment of all that he has is menaced by external forces or that those forces would impose intolerable conditions upon the exercise of his skill and labour. Therefore he must risk his life in order that he may thereby do what he can to safeguard his whole future. And so in its ultimate issue an unavoidable war becomes the supreme speculation in which all that one has and life itself are staked. Nor is this all. Present events give an unlooked-for definiteness to a speech of remarkable insight made by Dr Marshall in 1907. In it he discussed economic chivalry, connecting it with that chivalry of arms which is described by its historian as "having effected more than letters could accomplish in the ancient world; for it gave rise to the personal merit which in the knight, and in his successor, the gentleman of the present day, checks the pride of birth and the presumption of wealth[3]."

---

[1] "Essay on the Funding System" in *Works* (1852), p. 539.

[2] "Economic Calculus—Definitions—The first principle of Economics is that every agent is actuated only by self interest. The workings of this principle may be viewed under two aspects, according as the agent acts *without*, or *with*, the consent of others affected by his actions. In wide senses, the first species of action may be called *war*; the second, *contract*." *Mathematical Psychics*, 1881, pp. 16, 17.

[3] Charles Mills, *History of Chivalry*, II. p. 359.

Chivalry at its best inculcated the achievement of high emprise, the scorning of accidental advantages, the keeping of faith, protection of the weak and humility. So Dr Marshall envisages a chivalry in business which fosters public spirit and a delight in doing noble and difficult things because they are noble and difficult. "It includes a scorn for cheap victories and a delight in succouring those who need a helping hand. It does not disdain the gains to be won on the way, but it has the fine pride of the warrior who esteems the spoil of a well-fought battle, or the prizes of a tournament, mainly for the sake of the achievements to which they testify, and only in the second degree for the value at which they are appraised in the money of the market[1]." The inner importance of success is that it is "good *prima facie* evidence of leadership." "Men of this class," Dr Marshall continues, "live in constantly shifting visions, fashioned by their own brains, of various routes leading to the desired end; of the difficulties which nature will oppose to them on each route and of the contrivances by which they hope to get the better of her opposition[2]." In the ceaseless effort of man to express himself and to realise himself he is aware that the only way to make real and actual the thought which is conceived in his mind is to work it out as a fact in the world of things. He imagines a solution for some problem that confronts him, but the proof that his solution is valid can be best effected by actual trial. As it has been said—"the will is simply the man. Any act of will is the expression of the man as he at the time is. The motive issuing in his act, the object of his will, the idea which he sets himself to realise, are the same thing in different words....In willing he carries with him, so to speak, his whole self to the realisation of the given idea[3]."

War changes the circumstances in a tragic manner, but not the fundamental conditions. The quality of leadership is demonstrated where the stakes are the greatest. The sacrifice of comfort and ease which business exacts is demanded upon

[1] Marshall, "Economic Chivalry" in *Economic Journal*, XVII. p. 14.
[2] *Ibid.* p. 15.
[3] T. H. Green, *Prolegomena to Ethics*, 1890, p. 158.

a vastly larger scale but for the same end, namely the making objective the aim, subjectively conceived. But, if it be granted that this applies to those who are leaders in industry when they are forced to exchange the arts of peace for those of war, what is to be said of the position of the rank and file? Is there no chivalry for those, are they condemned to remain a more com-monalty? M. Maurice Barrès shows that ancient chivalry extended from the knights to the people, and he quotes the following significant saying:

Nul n'est vilains s'il ne fait vilenie.

He adds "c'est un vers des *Chansons de Geste*, comme ce pourrait être un vers de Corneille, comme c'est la pensée de chaque Français et Française en 1916[1]."

The British system also recognises the initiative of the private soldier and gives him opportunities. His efficiency resembles the pride of the craftsman in his work with the added conception of the spirit of co-operation and systematised effort. The same idea of combined struggle, which has long been a commonplace in the organisation of labour, is found both in the field and in the war-workshop. In the former it is gloriously common in the achievements of the battalion or the company, just as in the latter it shows itself in the pride which the platers and riveters of our shipyards take in the services of the ships they had helped to build at the battles of the Dogger Bank or off the coast of Jutland. Some commanders, reputed great, have dealt with their troops as Omar Khayyám imagined that Destiny dealt with man:

'Tis all a Chequer-board of Nights and Days
Where Destiny with Men for Pieces plays:
　　Hither and thither moves, and mates, and slays,
And one by one back in the Closet lays[2].

Rather in the modern British system, soldiers are recognised as men, not as inanimate pieces in a vast war game, and their individual responsibility and initiative are encouraged. Hence they feel they have an active share in the achievements in which

---

[1] M. Barrès, *Le Blason de la France*, 1916, p. 15.
[2] FitzGerald's Translation (Edition 1).

they participate. Modern chivalry in war was well described during Marlborough's campaigns by a writer in *The Spectator.* "The fine gentleman in that band of men is such a one as I have now in my eye, who is foremost in all danger to which he is ordered. His officers are his friends and companions as they are men of honour and gentlemen; the private men are his brethren, as they are of his species. They wish him in danger as he views their ranks, that they may have occasions to save him at their own hazard. Mutual love is the order of the files that he commands....Such is his regiment who knows mankind, and feels their distresses so as to prevent them[1]." It is from this spirit that there has been distilled that "fine extract, that pure essence which endures to all ages, while the grosser part, the residuum, may pass away and be lost in the course of time[2]."

Further, there is the same economic chivalry in the national service of non-combatants when, for instance, business men devote valuable time to serving, gratuitously, upon important committees which are concerned with functions in safeguarding the national interest. The same tendency is clearly observable when professional men (as for instance doctors) transfer their services to the State, not only at a considerably less remuneration than they had received previously, but also with grave risk to the future of their respective practices. Nor in this estimate should the extent of the largely unpaid work of women, in new and strange duties undertaken on behalf of the country, be overlooked.

These reflections have been confined of set purpose to considerations which are economic or which are derived from economic sources. It is almost needless to add that all that has been said is immensely strengthened by the moral and patriotic motives which move in the same direction with more sovereign power. And what the investigation of the present situation reveals is that the influence of the latter is not counteracted by economic desires and principles, but rather confirmed and increased.

---

[1] *The Spectator*, No. 152.
[2] *Speech by William Windham*, 22nd Dec. 1806.

When this reasoning is pressed to its logical conclusion, it may appear to encounter difficulties. One of these is the operation of the Military Service Act. If I may assume for a moment that the general line of argument is not received with dissent, I can well imagine the thoughts of some to take the direction that action which has an economic reference, even when it results in the undertaking of military service, must be assumed to be voluntary; but the case of the man, who did not attest and who is "deemed to have enlisted," involves his discharging duties against his will. To this it may be replied that some at least, and in all probability many, of those who came under the Military Service Act were in the apparently paradoxical position that, being conscripted, they undertook military duties which they themselves desired and thus their service was in essence voluntary. The apparent contradiction is resolved by the fact that these men held strongly that others of the same age and physique as themselves should perform similar national service. But this leaves a residuum of men who (apart from grounds of conscience) showed themselves reluctant to rise to the height which it was held the situation required. From one point of view this is a case in which the views of the majority must prevail against those of the minority, even to the extent of putting constraint upon the latter. From another it may fairly be contended that industrial freedom is far from being untrammelled. In a negative sense freedom may be enjoyed perhaps by one who lives the Cynic life of absence of desire, but for the normal man there are all the limitations which his station in life imposes on him. Thus the member of a Trade Union found his conditions of work determined for him in many ways. In certain cases he was not free to work for a specified employer, nor was he allowed to work upon certain conditions. As a rule, he may be held to have accepted the general policy of his Union; but, in several trades, the exercise of his skill was dependent upon his having joined the trade organisation. So what has happened in the war has been that a great national crisis has made it necessary to limit individual choice in certain directions in order to level up the service of citizens whose patriotism was distinctly below the average to the standard already achieved, voluntarily, by others who have been more far-seeing and alert. In other words, necessity has compelled the exaction of the same service from the laggards which the majority have offered of their own free will. Then measures to save the State demand fortitude and action which in other circumstances would be held to have been extreme. As Sir Walter Raleigh expressed it "in times of extremity, when resolution must be taken for the saving or utter loss of the State, then no regard is to be had of justice or injustice, mercy or cruelty, honour or ignominy, but rather, setting aside all respects, that course is to be followed which defends the lives and liberties of men[1]."

Compulsion does not cease with the provision of men for the forces. It affects the daily life of those who remain over in almost numberless ways under the Defence of the Realm Act and other emergency measures. Here it may appear that the organisation of commerce is fettered by a multitude of restrictions, though it should be noted, on the other side, there are cases in which pre-war restrictions have been removed temporarily. Thus it would appear that the economist is confronted with a new world, in which much is changed. First there came the dislocation of commerce caused by the outbreak of hostilities, and after that the State ordains rules, so that, in some trades, the merchant in effect ceases to be a merchant and becomes a quasi-bureaucrat.

It is in these circumstances that it has been hastily inferred that many economic generalisations have been abrogated. But in all the complexity of life it is impossible to state in detail all the conditions which are involved in a given situation. There are many that for long periods do not exert any important influence upon the effect which is investigated. A revolutionary change in the surroundings may suddenly force these neglected conditions into an unwonted prominence. It follows that what has happened is not that previous reasoning has been proved to be erroneous, but that elements in the chain of causation have

---

[1] Sir W. Raleigh, "The Cabinet Council" in *Works*, 1757, I. pp. 116, 117.

acquired new values. In a great war there is a change in relations between different social activities, and economic law occupies a new position when *Salus populi suprema est lex*. At the same time while national security, instead of being assumed, must be fought for with the greatest intensity, and in Adam Smith's language "defence is greater than opulence," under modern conditions opulence plays a striking part in the efficiency of defence. And so the relation between warlike and economic activity is a reciprocal one but under the governing condition that the latter is now directed in the main towards ends which are largely belligerent. Are we then to conclude that this economic activity is Protean in character—in time of peace being directed to the maintaining of peace and in time of war to the destructive energies of war? In other words, does the same activity at one time build up only to destroy its own work? This would be in effect a reversion to the doctrine of Herakleitus concerning the primal fire that consumes all things and from which again a new world is re-created[1].

This view, it seems to me, neglects the fruits of our past experience which, on the whole, has taught us that commerce tends towards peace amongst the nations rather than to war. To say that it furnishes means for war is not to imply that it is a necessary cause of war.

The essential lesson of industrial development is that its chief concern is in peace. But to secure a peace, which will be satisfactory, great sacrifices are demanded. And a full understanding of the situation is made difficult by the temporary separation of the standpoint of the individual and the nation. During war the attention and effort of the individual must be concentrated with the greatest intensity upon the present, that of the nation will be directed towards the larger outlook upon the future as it will be moulded by the momentous events now being transacted. It follows that for the time, but it is to be hoped only the time, the freedom of the individual must be absorbed in that of the national

---

[1] πυρός τ' ἀνταμείβεσθαι πάντα καὶ πῦρ ἁπάντων, ὥσπερ χρυσοῦ χρήματα καὶ χρημάτων χρυσός.

effort. His true and permanent interest is interwoven with that of his country. But in war it is impossible for the individual to determine the means by which this larger interest is to be advanced. Strategy, diplomacy and high finance all develop in secrecy during the actual conduct of hostilities. Thus the citizen must temporarily relinquish some of his rights as against the State, but only for his own future benefit. It is for these and similar reasons that in time of war industry becomes subject to a very large measure of governmental control. Wireless telegraphy and rapid communication have created new problems in the conduct of war, and the manufacturer or trader is cut off from many of the sources of intelligence upon which he was wont to rely in time of peace. Accordingly, instead of depending upon his own initiative and judgment, he must be directed, to a greater or less degree according to circumstances, upon the general plan which is only known in all its details to the responsible authorities. It is their function and duty to use the labour and other resources of the country in such a manner as they believe will best aid the accomplishment of the nation's aim.

There seems to be a popular way of thinking which is continually urging the Government to concentrate on the war and upon nothing else. Such advice—like much well-meant counsel—is directed in the wrong direction. It is the individual who should direct his life in this way during war time, by doing what is known to be of national importance under existing circumstances. But the Government of the country at the present time is in a peculiar sense the custodian of the future. It is responsible for this not only in the conduct of hostilities, but also in so far as the individual resigns to it his direction of his business concerns, and to that extent, at least, the Government becomes the trustee for the future of industry and social life. For the more effective conduct of hostilities the good citizen surrenders his own initiative ; but that power of freedom of industry and labour, which is temporarily in abeyance, must be conserved for the country when peace returns to it.

It is possible that there has been an unconscious common sense in the principle which has not as far as I am aware been formulated, but which appears to direct much of our war economics, namely for the Government to make changes in the economic system only when these are shown to be unavoidable for the more efficient prosecution of the war. There are violent contrasts in our economic life. In a diminishing number of instances it continues as in pre war times, in some it is modified by governmental interference, while in others it is transformed. Regarded apart from the past and the future, it is full of contradictions. Why should one man give up good wages and sustain the risks of active service for the relatively small army pay and allowances, while his neighbour, who is unfit for service, is securing higher earnings? Why should some make profits out of the present abnormal circumstances? Why should one man risk his career by accepting a commission in the army, while another makes a fortune by obtaining another kind of commission, namely to use his talents in the service of the State? Questions of this type could be multiplied almost indefinitely, and much argument would leave each conundrum much as it was when the discussion began. It appears to me that some confusion arises by considering the position as if it were static, whereas it is in reality a transition state towards something else. But what is that something else to be? Is it to be a state of war? because, if so, we cannot begin too soon to reform conditions which are anomalous if this is to be the world's destiny. On the contrary, the one great aspiration, which is shared alike by all the belligerents and by neutral nations, is for a stable and abiding peace. Therefore, regarding this as the goal, it may not be unwise to refrain from scrapping more of the economic arrangements of peace time than is unavoidable. It may be claimed for this method that there is a double economy of resources; first, during war, in saving the amount of labour which would be required for the establishing of a complete war-economy, and secondly in minimising the dislocation which will be involved in the transition from war organisation to peace organisation. The more complex the former, the greater the disturbance is likely to be. So that it seems sound practical wisdom to make emergency changes where these are shown to be desirable for military purposes, but not otherwise. Then the return of peace will find us with the essential parts of our industrial system ready to resume their former functions, instead of having to reconstruct them, perhaps under conditions of considerable difficulty.

These appear to be the governing factors in the industrial system in time of war. Naturally, precedence must be accorded to efficiency in the organising of the nation's resources for war. But, subject to this condition, the minimum amount of disturbance of the normal economic organisation is the wiser course.

It must not be overlooked that the success of the Navy has been remarkable in keeping open the routes for communication with countries overseas; and, in order to make full use of this goods must be produced to exchange for supplies drawn from foreign countries. This fact enables us—or at least should enable us—to avail ourselves of labour and capital at home, which could not otherwise be used for war purposes, in obtaining commodities useful for these ends by producing those goods which are necessary to be exchanged for them.

The strength of the British Empire may be represented as a majestic slow-moving force, which reaches its maximum momentum comparatively slowly. Because we were unprepared and because the resources are enormous the harnessing of these to war takes time. From the first preparations for hostilities until that maximum will be reached about five years would not be too long to complete a task of so great a magnitude. But the time which will be required to reach the maximum (if that be necessary) is in itself a testimony to the vastness and complexity of the resources with which we began—forces evoked from the man-power of all the Continents of the world, backed by the mobilised finance of the world's greatest money-power and supplied by the willing labour of a population which has always been foremost in the manufacturing arts. Such a force, as one imagines it, develops its greatest effectiveness only gradually, but it will have the fuller staying power.

This reasoning brings to light another condition which is implicit in the economic situation during war. War in all its sordidness seems inevitably to be material, and yet, in the present struggle, ideas are of supreme importance. Ultimately the real battle is between two opposed conceptions of life. We must be careful that in winning the war we do not lose the ideal for which we drew the sword. The British ideal is the Anglo-Saxon conception of freedom as opposed to the Germanic principle of State organisation, for which the State is everything and the individual nothing, which was described by Macaulay as being that "of all political fallacies which has perhaps had the widest and most mischievous operation[1]." During hostilities freedom is conceived as political, but the issue of the war will determine the governing principle of economic activity for a long time to come. The logical consequence of victory in war will be the maintaining of our industrial ideal of liberty, with its voluntary organisation and its development of individual initiative.

The maintaining of that ideal must not be understood to mean a return to the same conditions of industry which existed before the war. Freedom takes many forms in its details, and a nation obtains that type of liberty, political and industrial, which it has deserved. In our commercial and industrial organisation, as it existed during the first decade of the present century, there were many things which required amendment. The nation will emerge from this war poorer in material wealth but enriched in character. This will prove the necessary foundation for industrial and social advance. Our commercial machine had grown up very gradually and there were many parts in it which caused friction in its working. With clearer vision and a wider outlook, it will be possible to reform much and to improve much. When the smoke of battle clears away, when submarines no longer disturb the depths of the sea and air-craft cease to vex the calm stillness of the upper air with the rattle of their guns, men will return to the arts of peace which they were forced to abandon for those of war. They will return to

---

[1] "Essay on Machiavelli" in *Essays*, 1885, p. 48.

us having learnt much, and perchance having forgotten something. The task before them will be the reaping of the full fruit of their perils and their toils in recreating industry and commerce in a manner which will be worthy of them and of their race. We shall have bought peace and security at a very great price, but that price should bring a bonus eventually in a better and more efficient industry. As yet it is possible to see only its general character, but not its details; just as one views a city in the far distance. It will, I think, be less sordid than the industry of the past; free, too, but with a well-ordered freedom. Efficiency, both of men and machines, can be increased, while, if this is accomplished, the condition of workers will be better. Production, also, will be larger, for after a long period of somnolence, the nation will be more awakened and alert. What is more important, the quality and conditions of production will be improved, and it is to be hoped that the old pride of the craftsman in his work will return in an intensified form and will manifest itself on a much greater scale, for it will be reinforced by the whole strength of an improved and extended organisation of industry.

It may seem that this tentative forecast involves a certain degree of economic faith. And this is justified at an epoch when, in the graphic phrase of Sir Thomas More, "things are in so great a fermentation[1]," and spiritual forces are freed from the restraints that clogged their activities. This is a psychological basis upon which to build and it is confirmed by past experience. The revivifying effect of the Napoleonic wars was anticipated by Chalmers and confirmed after the event by Tooke. The first wrote in 1794 after the outbreak of hostilities "I engage to maintain that what has happened in our former wars will again happen in the present war in a greater or less degree; that we shall lose some of our external commerce, while we shall probably gain the extent of our losses from some other source, that the spring of our trade may be pressed down by the prevalence of war, but will rebound on the return of peace; that our domestic industry will be little affected by distant hostilities,

[1] *Utopia*, 1737, p. 29.

whilst consumption will run on in its usual channel without the obstructions of warfare; and that, upon the restoration of tranquillity, enterprising people of this happy land will carry the energy, which they have ever derived from war, into the usual avocations of peace; so as to have hereafter, as they have uniformly had, more trade and more shipping and ampler means of acquiring wealth when hostilities shall cease than they had when they were goaded into unprovoked hostilities by a restless enemy[1]." In parts of Chalmers' forecast we may note cases where events did not follow the course he anticipated, though often in exceeding rather than in falling short of his expectations. Thirty years afterwards, when Tooke reviewed the great struggle, he pointed out that a state of war diminishes the supply of commodities, but that there are counteracting causes, amongst which he mentions the increased activity, industry and intelligence in the great mass of the population remaining, so that as much or even more may be produced than before; increased accumulation of capital; improvements in agriculture and machinery tending to increase production with the same or less capital and labour. And he concludes that "all these circumstances concurred in this country during the whole of the late contest, and the consequence was an increase of production and population in spite of the opposite tendency arising out of a state of war[2]." This is confirmed by another contemporary observer—Joseph Lowe, who spoke of the "late war" as having "involved a sacrifice of property not inferior to the sacrifice of lives. To this double drain on our resources what has been the grand counterpoise? Our progress in the arts of peace: the power of extracting a larger subsistence from the soil; a larger revenue from our labour and capital[3]."

Present conditions do not appear to justify any less courage in facing the future of commerce than that shown by Chalmers

[1] G. Chalmers, *An Estimate of the Comparative Strength of Great Britain,* 1794, p. xxi.

[2] T. Tooke, *Thoughts and Details on the High and Low Prices from* 1793 *to* 1822 (1824), p. 209.

[3] J. Lowe, *The Present State of England in regard to Agriculture, Trade and Finance,* 1824, p. 292.

over a century ago. A calm, but at the same time a balanced confidence in what is to come will be most in accord with the new forces which are even now coming into operation. If we make good use of these, there is much more to be hoped than to be feared.

The energising of the nation through the time of trial will result in greater efficiency when the present struggle is ended. Discoveries of new processes and methods, with improvements in old ones, will lead not only to a more productive industry; but, it is to be hoped, also to a better industry. Europe will awake from the nightmare of armaments with which it has been too long oppressed. As the murk of the battle cloud clears one sees the first signs of a fairer dawn in which the arts of industry, broadened and deepened and at the same time more humanely organised, can accomplish in the next generation more than even was dreamt of by the discoverers of the great Victorian era. And further, great as these gains may be they will be surpassed by more immaterial improvements. The general quickening of the national spirit may be expected to lead in the end to greater national unity and ultimately perhaps to more international co-operation. Thus it will be possible to obtain eventually the full fruits of peace in greater harmony both at home, and also by the securing of that long-continued amity amongst nations which commerce requires for its stable and regular development.

"FOR THE DURATION OF
THE WAR"

Assiduo labuntur tempora motu
Non secus ac flumen. Neque enim consistere flumen,
Nec levis hora potest: sed ut unda impellitur unda,
Urgeturque prior venienti, urgetque priorem,
Tempora sic fugiunt pariter, pariterque sequuntur;
Et nova sunt semper. Nam quod fuit ante, relictum est;
Fitque quod haud fuerat: momentaque cuncta novantur.

OVID.

"FOR THE DURATION OF THE WAR"

From 1917 back to 1492 seems a far cry, but in that year there was printed in English at Antwerp by Gerard Leeu a version of the *Dyalogus or Communyng betwixt Salomon and Marcolphus*. A few sentences from this quaint mediaeval discussion may serve as an introduction to the subject of the present lecture. It may be premised that the sayings of Solomon in the dialogue may be supposed to represent the wisdom of the wise, while the retorts of Marcolphus, who was "right rude and great of body but right subtyll and wyse of wyt," indicate the comment of shrewd, untutored common sense. With the apparent inconsequence which characterises the dialogue, after counsels by Solomon and sarcastic comments by Marcolphus upon learning, self-praise, and the training of the young, the discussion proceeds:

Salo. All maner kyndes turne agen to theyre furste nature.
Mar. A worne tabyll cloth turnyth agen to his furste kynde[1].

Both the aphorism of Solomon and particularly the rejoinder to it show the peculiarly static conception of social phenomena during the Middle Ages, and one wonders how far it finds a parallel in the modern expedient of making changes for the duration of the war in the apparent expectation that when peace comes the clock can be put back; and, in the words put in the mouth of Solomon, things will "turne agen to theyre furste nature." But what will happen if, in the metaphor of the homely critic, the institutions have become worn and

---

[1] *This is the Dyalogus or Communyng betwixt the wyse king Salomon and Marcolphus* (facsimile, 1892).

obsolete, how can the "worne tabyll cloth" patch its own holes? Indeed, may we not further ask, if some part of our industrial or social system had shown itself to be imperfect before the war, why should it be replaced after the war with the original holes, as the Indian tailor is said sometimes to copy a garment given him as a pattern by reproducing all the defects of wear or accident in the original?

Even under assumed static conditions the difficulties of emergency measures for the duration of the war are great. Those conditions however represent in reality an artificial simplification of the problem. Industrial life is essentially dynamic, and it may be most fitly compared to an organism. It is impossible to immobilise any part or function of an organism without producing compensating activities in it, and the change is likely to be the greater the more abnormal the circumstances are. Acceptances and bills of exchange may be "placed in cold storage," but this applies to the actual documents. The activities of international trade, of which they were the instruments, must either cease or else be supplied from some other source. Whatever attempt is made to isolate and immobilise a particular function, the process of adaptation to environment continues; and therefore, even if the use of that particular function is temporarily suspended by governmental regulation, it will be found impossible to restore it to precisely the same work which it formerly performed and in the same manner, because other parts of the organism and its surroundings will have changed. Further, there is always the possibility that, during the interval of suspension, some other organ will have endeavoured to adapt itself to the function previously exercised by the first. In addition another condition may be expected. The catastrophic circumstances of war produce new economic phenomena, and the industrial organism at once begins to adapt itself to these. Thus new functions are acquired, often by existing organs undertaking changed functions, or some new organs may appear. Once these have been established they will tend to persist, only falling gradually into disuse if the conditions after the war make it impossible for them to continue. And so, upon this hypothesis, some—and it may be much—waste of economic energy appears possible in the first years of peace, so that the whole position, as affected by emergency economic measures, requires more detailed analysis than it has yet received.

In circumstances of crisis, danger or under abnormal conditions, "when the work of years is crowded in a single hour[1]," time appears to be as it were *stretched out*, owing probably to the many experiences which are forced into it and the insistence with which they press themselves upon the attention. Thus the rush of experiences extends time, as De Quincey has shown[2], and a period which seems short when marked on the calendar appears to be very remote. In this way the early days of the war seem already to be far away, and in one sense almost to have become matters of history. For this reason some of the emergency measures are even now almost forgotten, either because they were withdrawn or because people soon became habituated to them and gradually accepted them without recalling their original emergency character. These various steps during the first two years and a half of war fall naturally into several distinct groups. First there were provisions which were designed to prevent a crisis on the outbreak of hostilities. It has been hinted that possibly less interference might have sufficed[3], but there seems sound wisdom, backed by the teaching of history, in Ricardo's dictum that a crisis is likely when a country emerges from a long peace into a state of war[4], and all the more if the latter comes suddenly. The second group consisted of a variety of measures related to agreements with Trades Unions, whereby the customs of the latter were relaxed in order to facilitate recruiting by introducing labour to replace that diverted to undertake military service. The majority of the agreements between employers and employed are for the duration of the war, though others

[1] Dow, *Sethona*, Act II.   [2] De Quincey, *Works*, 1862, I. p. 259.
[3] Keynes, "War and the Financial System," *Economic Journal*, xxiv. p. 483.
[4] Ricardo, *Works*, 1852, p. 160.

are to terminate as the men displaced return and are available for their former work. Closely connected with these are the further developments required for the dilution of labour. Next come all the orders arising directly out of a state of hostilities, most of which, but by no means all of them, may be grouped under the measures against Trading with the Enemy[1] and for the Defence of the Realm[2]. A separate and miscellaneous class comprises changes in the social and economic system which arose either out of the foregoing acts, proclamations or orders or from the war itself. Finally in the third year of the war action by the State in relation to the food supply of the country with which the question of transport (particularly by sea) was connected became so important as to constitute a distinct group.

As has already been shown, military reasons have involved great and widespread interference by the State with the pre-war conditions of trade. The forces consume many more commodities than in previous wars; and thus the schedule of goods, which the Entente Powers by their command of the sea endeavour in their own interest to deny to the enemy, tends to grow longer and longer. Added to this, there is the existence of the blockade of Germany, which is complicated by the transit trade through the adjoining neutral countries. As a consequence, freedom of exporting commodities must be rigorously supervised. It follows that one of the great advantages of our cause, by a curious paradox, results in a limitation of trade which is greater than if we had been weaker. This is a permanent condition as old as strategy and as unchanged as the sea itself. Its effects have been described by Coleridge in a passage of great power, written during the Napoleonic war, which applies almost word for word to the struggle with Germany. "Surely," he wrote during the days of the Continental System, "never from the beginning of the world was such a tribute of admiration paid by one power to another, as Buonaparte within the last few years has paid to the British Empire! With all the natural

---

[1] Proclamation Aug. 5, 1914, No. 1252 et seq.
[2] 4 and 5 Geo. V, c. 29.

and artificial powers of almost the whole of continental Europe, with all the fences and obstacles of all public and private morality broken down before him, with a mighty Empire of fifty millions of men, nearly two thirds of whom speak the same language, and are as it were fused together by the intensest nationality; with this mighty and swarming Empire, organised in all its parts for war, and forming one huge camp, and himself combining in his own person the two-fold power of monarch and commander-in-chief; with all these advantages, with all these stupendous instruments and inexhaustible resources of offence, this mighty being finds himself imprisoned by the enemy he most hates and would fain despise, insulted by every wave that breaks upon his shores, and condemned to behold his vast flotillas as worthless and idle as the sea weed that rots around their keels[1]!"

War causes enormous diversion of labour. It was not only for the manning of the long lines of siege-works which at one period encircled the Central Powers, but also for the supply of the manifold needs of the Navy and the Army that a force behind the fighting front must be mobilised. And this has been effected by action of the State in very large measure. Adam Smith estimated that in his time the civilised States of Europe could not support as soldiers without ruin more than one per cent. of their populations[2]. The progress of mechanical invention and the accumulation of wealth have made it possible to maintain much greater numbers in the field. Before the present war it was usually taken as a basis of calculation that a continental country could mobilise ten per cent. of its population. That proportion has certainly been largely exceeded during the present contest, but by how much will not be known until after peace has been made. Up to the present, estimates, believed to be well informed, have placed the percentages reached by some of the belligerents at 16. Whether this high proportion can in Adam Smith's phrase be maintained "without ruin by the country which employs them," is a matter which

[1] Coleridge, *The Friend*, Section I. Essay VII. (Ed. 1867, p. 146).
[2] A. Smith, *Wealth of Nations* (ed. Cannan), II. p. 191.

only the future can determine. It is however significant that Plutarch puts into the mouth of Hannibal the saying that unless he could bring Fabius Maximus to battle, he must be defeated in the end owing to the superiority of the Romans in men and resources. In view of the great, and perhaps the extreme mobilisations, it is clear that there is an important advantage upon the side of that combination of Powers which is able to keep its forces adequately supplied for the longer period. This fact is an important one, and it has a bearing upon emergency measures which will call for discussion later.

Diversion of labour involves replacement of labour, but it must be in the right direction. By the third year of war the belligerent countries between them may be calculated to have mobilised between 40 millions and 50 millions of men for naval and military service. To this immense total some addition must be made for the increase in the forces of neutral countries. So far as all these were not professional soldiers and were workers there is a gross loss to the world's production. That however is not a net loss, if it had been the war would soon have ended. The displaced labour is partly replaced by great employment of women, by retired men returning to work, by increased use of machinery, by greater efficiency and finally, in varying degrees, by the setting prisoners of war and subject populations to forced labour. Still emergency labour cannot fill the whole gap in the general production and the shortage will be unequally distributed between different industries. Those, which supply the technical needs of war, exercise a paramount demand both for labour and materials; and, therefore, the deficiency is felt more severely amongst the remainder. At this stage the facilitating transfer of labour by governmental action became necessary, and almost simultaneously the third year of war brought a new problem. While the production of commodities, with the exception of munitions and goods of a similar character, was decreased, consumption in the United Kingdom of those goods was not proportionately diminished. Then there came the season of 1916–17 during which crops were short. This is a phenomenon which has marked the progress of many previous great wars, almost as if Nature were determined to endeavour to force peace by starving the combatants. In all probability the effect of an unfavourable season is accentuated by a scarcity of agricultural labour, destruction of food and scarcity of means of transport. Thus several circumstances concurred to induce State action in the directing of labour and the control of food supplies.

This, however, is only one side of an exceedingly complex problem. In so far as sea-routes are open, the Allied Powers are in the position of being able to employ neutral labour to supplement that of their own people. This supplementing is complete for the period of the war when payment for goods purchased abroad is made by a foreign loan. The process in fact resolves itself into a borrowing of the commodities. But a sounder method is to pay for such goods as it is necessary to import by means of exports, and this again requires the allocation of labour to produce the exports. So it follows that wide and comprehensive regulation by the State both of labour-power and of consumption was considered necessary.

At this stage of the argument some points of interest, perhaps mainly theoretical, emerge. In so far as the State effects a transfer of labour from any type of production which is judged less necessary in the national interest to another which is more necessary, it may have to face a loss of revenue from the lessened taxable capacity of the transferred labour in its new employment. Suppose for instance that a woman's "beauty doctor," who returned her income from her occupation as £1,000 a year, is diverted to the making of munitions at which she earns only a fraction of the former amount, it is clear that, in the first instance, the State by reason of the transfer will secure less from her both in direct and indirect taxation. But this is not a final result. The phenomenon has an influence on the revenue both forwards and backwards. The remainder of her former income was expended in various ways and will have yielded profits to those who supplied the goods and services which she demanded. Once the "beauty-parlour" is given up, all those who employed her services are left with a surplus income to be expended in other directions (whence the State can derive revenue) or alternatively it may be possible to intercept it directly in the form of taxation. Therefore the apparent loss is largely reduced, but not altogether. In highly specialised employment the immaterial wealth in the acquired skill may be temporarily wasted with resulting loss. But that loss might not be so great as one would anticipate. Thus instead of setting this woman to make munitions, it might be possible, if she had real skill, to employ it in attending to soldiers who had been partially disfigured by wounds. In fact the success of transfer of labour will depend upon the utilisation of any acquired aptitudes in some thing that is specifically war work.

The transfer of labour to produce goods for export has problems of its own. Suppose, for instance, that it takes the form of exchanging British goods manufactured under conditions of Increasing Return for foreign goods which were made under conditions of Diminishing Return. Here the military and the economic problems must be distinguished. It may be granted that the commodities exported have no value for military purposes, while those imported are important from this standpoint. From the economic point of view it might appear that in the exchange we are, in fact, giving more labour for less labour; and therefore, if the goods in question could be supplied in sufficient quantities at home, it would seem to follow that labour could be used to better advantage in the making of them here. But in this case, as so often elsewhere in the study of war conditions, we have to deal with short periods only. Ultimately, in manufacturing industries the labour required for producing machinery has to be taken into account, while in the short war period the machinery is already in existence. Indeed, taking into account the slow but none the less real diversion of demand from luxuries, the tendency would have been for machinery to be left idle, which was formerly employed to meet this demand, unless it had been used to supply the export trade.

The mobilisation of industry under the direction of the

Government is *ipso facto* intended to be for the duration of the war. It will, however, have important after-effects. In the words of Burke "war never leaves where it found a nation." "For the duration," as the soldiers succinctly put it[1], may mean much in the determination of the state of industry and social life in the years of peace. How far this will happen will depend upon the spirit in which the present and future changes are effected. It is said that James I called for his old shoes because they were easiest, and many of us face the upheaval of war with old ways of thinking, because they are easiest, and we have so long been accustomed to them. This is in effect the fatal attempt to live in two worlds of thought at the same time to which the satire of Terence may be applied when he speaks of an attempt to rave rationally[2]. But there is an extreme upon the other side, which starts from the conception of this war as "unparalleled" and "unprecedented," and takes practical measures by making a series of fresh starts, as if mankind had been plunged into a new existence. It is unlikely that this course is the best for the main object of securing a victorious decision in battle, and it would react unfavourably upon the future of industry and commerce. The trained faculty of economic analysis can be applied to the new circumstances, as to the old, not by using former generalisations, but by an examination of the fresh phenomena with a view to ascertaining their real meaning, that being precisely the element in the situation which is liable to be apprehended wrongly by the casual observer. Further, for a nation which has fought many victorious wars in the past we have strangely ignored the assistance which our history could have given us.

---

[1] The following is an extract from a conversation of a war correspondent with a soldier in Mesopotamia. "I was surprised at the loyalty the 'sausage' evoked. It was more than professional interest; it amounted almost to affection. I asked a private in the L——s how he liked his new work. 'I wouldn't mind taking on this 'ere job for the duration,' he told me." *Times*, December 20, 1916.

[2]   Nihilo plus agas,
Quam si des operam, ut cum ratione insanias.
Eunuchus, Act I. Sc. I.

This defect has been urged at the same time by Dr Cunningham as regards Economic History[1], and by Count Charles de Souza as regards Military History. The comment of the latter as an unprejudiced outsider, but at the same time an enthusiastic admirer, is particularly interesting. "The British," he writes, "in spite of their love for tradition, have another and a more detrimental tendency than the one above stated; they are prone to disregard the teachings of history[2]." The "teaching" of history, however, requires to be most carefully interpreted, at least as regards commerce. It is the experience of the past, but at the same time it is often difficult to discern the extent to which it applies to the present. It is always necessary to discover which are the significant events in the two sets of circumstances and afterwards to enquire the extent to which they are similar. It is only then that the lesson, if lesson there be, can be assimilated and perhaps applied in practice. Hence we are not so much concerned with parallels, as with a species of analogical reasoning, resembling to some extent that employed in Bishop Butler's *Analogy of Religion*, but used in a reverse direction.

As yet we stand too near epoch-making events to be able to discern their true import, though

> the soul is a rock that abides,
> But her ears are vexed with the roar and her face with the
> foam of the tides.

Yet it may perhaps be guessed that, when the historian of the future comes to understand it all, he will be impressed most with the immensity of the voluntary effort of the country, not only in the undertaking of military service but in vast numbers everywhere doing what they could for the common cause. There is a most remarkable passage in the speech which Mazzini delivered in 1848 upon the death of the brothers Bandiera. It runs "the Angel of Martyrdom and the Angel of

---

[1] Cunningham, *Progress of Capitalism in England*, 1916, pp. viii, 26, 27.
[2] De Souza, *Germany in Defeat, Third Phase*, 1916, p. 135.

Victory are brothers; but the one looks up to heaven, and the other looks down to the earth, and it is only when, from epoch to epoch, their eyes meet between earth and heaven, that creation is embellished with a new life, and a people arises, evangelist and prophet, from the cradle or the tomb." As the Roman soldiers, who had undermined the temple at Veii (which was then besieged) heard the priest proclaiming that "the Gods offer victory to him who shall finish this sacrifice," they seized and carried the entrails to Camillus who completed the rite: so superiority in continuing to sacrifice to the end will be the earnest of final and complete success in the present contest. It has been the greatness and at the same time the intensely concentrated character of the war which made the freewill offering of the people, vast as this was beyond anything previously imagined, not yet sufficient, and compulsion had to be added. There remained some who might have replied to the calls and advice of the Government and of the Food Controller in the words of the song of Hassan of Bassorah in the *Arabian Nights*:

> Censor of me, leave blame and stint advice!
> Thou bringest wearying words and wisdom vain.

It is probable that, even if voluntary sacrifice had been altogether adequate, instead of not quite adequate, the State would have required to exercise functions, unusual to it, in order to organise the services offered. The need for compulsory powers made such action inevitable. It is at this point that special care must be taken in regard to the future of industry. The national conscience feels that this war is one for liberty. And to ensure success the individual resigns his personal freedom for the time to the State in order to aid in achieving the common aim. The State thus becomes in a very special sense the trustee of the liberty of the people:

> 'Twas a large trust, and must be managed nicely[1].

That trust resembles one of the most solemn acts of a regiment before it goes on active service, namely when it places

---

[1] Otway, *The Orphan*, Act II. Sc. I.

its flags in the safe keeping of a Church or of that body which it most reveres. In the same way the Government has become the depositary of the liberties of the greater part of the nation. This process will tend to produce consequences which may lead to dangerous economic results. Under a system of State-regulation of industry, initiative must be checked. In very many cases the merchant and the worker cannot employ their respective energies in the manner which seems best to them. Instead of acting as each considers most advantageous, he must proceed under direction from outside, and so there is the danger that habits of dependence may replace those of alert enterprise. In so far as this is a risk, it is one which must be taken in view of the vast issue which is at stake, and it constitutes what might be described as one of the "invisible" sacrifices of the war. Clearly it should be minimised as far as possible by refraining from pledging the future of commercial and industrial freedom to a greater extent than is absolutely unavoidable. But this is not the only possibility. It may be that experience of governmental restraint has set up a counter-tendency, none the less powerful because at present inarticulate. Patriotic men everywhere abstain from criticism and complaint, recognising that there may be important facts connected with the conduct of the war with which they are not acquainted; and, even when their judgment condemns governmental action, they console themselves with the reflection that it is only for the duration of the war. Thus, upon this hypothesis, the declaration of peace will release a strong counter-tendency, which might easily be carried to extremes. On the other side, governmental control tends in itself to establish a species of vested interests, which will press for their continuance. In imagining an extension of State-activity, not much more than that which exists at present, J. S. Mill was of opinion that not "all the freedom of the press and popular constitution of the legislature would make this or any other country free otherwise than in name. And the evil would be greater, the more efficiently and scientifically the administrative machinery was constructed—the more skilful the arrangements for obtaining the best qualified hands and heads with which to work it[1]." Though Mill's fears may have been extreme, there is more than a substratum of truth in his pessimism. What is required at the present time is to refrain from taking action, as far as is possible, which would, if taken, determine the future. Often there are several ways of effecting a given aim, and it is desirable that, when there is such a choice, the future freedom of initiative should not be curtailed; while on the other side, in so far as State-action has shown itself beneficial, the way should be left open to use it in limited fields when peace has been secured.

Grotius points out that serenity of mind in the conduct of war cannot be retained, unless attention is paid to the ultimate attainment of peace[2]. But peace after this war will differ from the peace before it, and that will have an effect upon the immediate future of commerce, particularly in foreign trade. Much fury has been added to the fire, and the hysteria of hate cannot pass away immediately, "National dislike easily and quickly transfers itself from the field of battle to that of commerce[3]." Such passion, as Bacon said long ago in adapting a metaphor of Seneca, is "like ruin which breaks itself upon that on which it falls[4]." It is unfortunate that the self-destruction of hate is not accomplished at once—it is a slow suicide which only ends after long years. To hope that future trading relations with enemy nations will be amicable for some years to come would be to display an ill-informed optimism. The nation has a right to demand security for the industry of its people, and to see that any resources which are judged vital for its safety are managed by its own subjects, or, at least, are not under foreign control. But an impartial examination of the situation is likely to show that the quantity of industry affected will not be very great. Apart from this, feelings of resentment occasioned by the grievous wrongs which we have suffered may be expected to urge a trade policy which will differ-

---

[1] J. S. Mill, *On Liberty*, 1887, p. 65.
[2] Grotius, *De Jure Belli et Pacis*, xxv. 2.
[3] Clark, *Proposed Customs Union of the British Empire*, 1898, p. 9.
[4] Bacon, *Works*, 1765, I. p. 522.

entiate against the products of recently hostile nations. This is only natural, and the impulse will be supported by one type of thought which had become prominent before the war. So far as this spirit prevails, it will mean an aggressive policy in external trade and extensive State-interference with it. At the present stage dogmatism upon one side or the other would be unwise, indeed in the past this whole subject has suffered from dogmatic treatment. We must be prepared to face facts and to deal with them as wisely as may be. The bias of ill-feeling left by the war will be towards limitation of foreign trade with Germany in particular. It will be impossible to confine differentiation; and, in so far as it will be established, it may be likely to extend. Prohibitions, protections, subsidies and guarantees, all result in directing commerce into channels which are believed to be politically advantageous. If a political advantage cannot be shown, the well-worn free trade arguments, in my judgment, still apply. But the estimation of political advantage will be extraordinarily difficult, for the distinguishing of it will be distorted by the remaining elements of rancour and bad feeling. As yet we do not know precisely what was the extent and the consequences of the so-called German policy of peaceful penetration. Much should depend upon what will ultimately have been proved as to its real nature. For some years, until the efficacy of the guarantees of a lasting peace have been tested by time, it would be the height of folly to run any avoidable risks. Thus the problem contains a large element which is purely political, and all that the economist can do is to point out that temporary conditions will be upon the side of State-interference. Besides the smouldering fires of national resentment, there will be the immediate recollection of the horror of war and the firm conviction that nothing possible will be wanting in national preparedness. Closer relations with our Allies, who rely more upon State-action than we have been in the habit of doing, will also exert an influence, and the probable future partnership of the Dominions will operate in the same direction. The war will have lasted long enough to habituate people's minds to the environment of hostilities, and they will not be able to divest themselves of their whole mental outlook just because peace has been proclaimed.

War economics are mainly, though not altogether, dominated by the consideration of "short periods." The wider aspects of post-war phenomena will involve the broader vision of the "long period." Here a fundamental condition will be the new exigencies of national defence, particularly in providing for an adequate naval strength. It may be anticipated that this will lead to a much closer collaboration of the Dominions and Possessions both in policy and financial responsibility, while the latter will react upon commerce. One method by which this object might be attained would be the establishment of a Customs Union for the British Empire, and those parts of it which at present derive most of their revenue from import duties could easily adapt themselves to the change. The correlate of a Customs Union would be a freer trade within the Empire; which in process of time might develop into inter-Imperial free trade. Even before the present war Professor Nicholson, who spoke from the free trade standpoint, wrote as follows: "If, then, a Customs Union could be adopted by the British Empire with a provision for the assignment of a certain proportion of the yield for Imperial purposes, especially defence, it would be absurd to object merely on the ground of the difficulty of imposing equivalent excises. Internal free trade throughout the Empire, though possible without any Customs Union, would be promoted and strengthened thereby, and the benefits of real commercial union are too great to be cast aside on account of a literal interpretation of free trade, which is as little defensible as the literal interpretation of a scriptural text badly translated from the original[1]." Such "a Customs Union for the whole British Empire would be the most powerful instrument that ever existed, if it could be used effectively, either for commercial agreements or for retaliation[2]." This view is based on one of the two "Utopian" schemes of Adam

---

[1] Nicholson, *A Project of Empire*, 1909, p. 264. It may be noted that this scheme included other taxes besides Customs duties.

[2] *Ibid.* p. 265.

Smith[1] (the other having been his recommendation of free
trade for Great Britain), and I refer to this "golden dream"
of an Empire in actuality rather than "in imagination" in
order to eliminate the feelings of anger which cannot fail to
exist during a war such as this has been and are likely to survive
for some years as an aftermath of the struggle.   That forecast,
it will be noticed, is founded, not upon passion, but upon the
fundamental needs of defence.   From the economic point of
view it is reinforced by the prospects of commercial agreements
with the Allied nations.   Thus, if consolidation of the Empire
proceeded by this method, there would be a loss of freedom of
external trade in one direction and a gain in another direction.
Changes in foreign relations have made great and important
additions to the list of the Allied nations, and thus the proportion
of our pre-war trade which was carried on with countries now
united with us has become much larger since the beginning of
the war.   This is open to possible commercial agreements in
addition to the suggested Imperial Customs Union.   But the
magnitude of the trade affected will, in all probability, make
the framing of such agreements, in the event of the task
being attempted, more complex.   Much will depend upon the
character of the peace which will be secured, namely whether
it will be one which will render a continuance of a species of
mobilisation of commerce necessary, or, upon the contrary,
whether that will not be necessary.   In any case, it is probable
that, for some time to come, commerce with countries lately
hostile will be subject to limitation; while, upon the hypothesis
of a Customs Union and commercial agreements, there would
probably be a reduction in trade with the few nations which
will remain neutral until the end of the war.   Also the obscure,
though none the less important, effect upon the shipping industry must not be lost sight of.   As yet it is difficult to estimate
the balance of economic gain or loss, whether it will incline
to one side or to the other.   As for the political advantage,
it may be the political necessity, that is for the statesman to
determine.   In the words of the economist, whose work these

[1] A. Smith, *Wealth of Nations* (ed. Cannan), II. p. 419.

lectures commemorate, "The legislator is neither chemist, nor physicist, nor physician, nor economist, nor moralist, but all of these in some degree, and something more as well, in the sense that he must gather to a focus the complex calculus of probabilities, the data for which are supplied by the separate investigators[1]." More than in the past a well-balanced judgment will be required, something which will be sound, sane and impersonal like the φρόνιμος of Aristotle with at the same time that rare quality of political intuition that divines the future. The latter is to be sharply distinguished from those who frame merely attractive schemes which, while grandiose in conception, fail when tested by reality. The difference is well expressed in the lines of Savage:

> Men, wild of brain by heated fancy swayed
> 'Stead of sage judgment; judgment, that of old
> Has founded, modelled, rendered empires great,
> And settled standard laws[2].

The future of external trade cannot be developed further until in the next lecture something has been said about the character of the commerce of a maritime power, but there still remains one aspect of freedom of commerce which calls for comment. In the discussions of the organisation of trade during the early years of the present century one aspect of the subject received undue prominence. Free trade, from the politician's point of view, meant absence of duties upon British imports: free trade from the economic point of view means the maximum commercial and industrial opportunity both in trade at home and overseas. Production at home can be made much more free. It has been restrained by much inertness, and also by many conventions and customs which are anachronisms in the world of to-day and which, if they were continued, would be serious impediments in the world of to-morrow. Also, it is to be hoped that the period of emergency restraint of trade will not leave any unnecessary survivals when industry

---

[1] W. S. Jevons, *The State in Relation to Labour*, 1882, p. 29.
[2] Savage, *Sir Thomas Overbury*, Act I.

has readjusted itself after the war. Great Britain took up arms in defence of liberty, and it would be one of the most tragic ironies of history if we secured political freedom for oppressed nations on the field and found that freedom of industry had been partly lost at home. Knowledge, application and judgment should be effective in securing to the nation the immaterial fruits of its trials; so that the fine spirit of achievement in circumstances of the greatest difficulty and danger may have free play in resuming the material development which was arrested by the war.

COMMUNICATIONS OF A
MARITIME STATE

Kept than the sea about in speciall,
Which of England is the towne wall.
As though England were likened to a citie,
And the wall environ were the sea.
Kepe then the sea that is the wall of England:
And than is England kept by Goddes hande;
That as for any thing that is without,
England were at ease withouten doubt,
And thus should every lond one with another
Entercommon, as brother with his brother,
And live togither werreless in unitie,
Without rancour in very charity,
In rest and peace, to Christes great pleasance,
Without strife, debate and variance.

Libel of English Policie, exhorting all England to keepe
the Sea (written about 1437).

COMMUNICATIONS OF A
MARITIME STATE

During the wars of the French Revolution the aged philosopher Kant wrote his essay on a perpetual peace, an ideal which he described as no mere empty dream, but as a problem which, by approximating solution little by little would, at length, accomplish its aim[1]. It needed no little courage to enunciate this ideal at the time, and Kant was so conscious of this that he began his treatise by a reference to the place where he had found his title. It was the inscription upon a picture of a cemetery. And he goes on to say that in the wars which will happen before the coming of that peace which will be unbroken, no combatant should use such barbarous methods as would render mutual confidence impossible at the cessation of hostilities, else the end can be nothing but a mere truce, to be followed by a war of extermination which would indeed establish a perpetual peace—but only in a vast cemetery of the human race. Rather he would aim as his ideal at the precept, "Search first the kingdom of pure practical reason with its justice and this other thing (namely perpetual peace) will be added unto you." Of late years it has been the fashion amongst certain classes in Germany to regard Kant's treatise as the result of senility. One recalls Nietzsche's address to the warrior, "Let your peace be a victory! Say ye that a good cause will hallow even war? I say unto you a good war halloweth everything....And when your soul waxeth great, it waxeth haughty, and in your exaltation there is wickedness[2]." The element of

[1] First printed in 1795.
[2] Euer Friede sei ein Sieg!

Ihr sagt, die gute Sache sei es, die sogar den Krieg heilige? Ich sage euch: der gute Krieg ist es, der jede Sache heiligt....Und wenn eure Seele gross wird, so wird sie übermüthig, und in eurer Erhabenheit ist Bosheit.

Also sprach Zarathustra, 1893, p. 63.

wickedness in the infliction of avoidable suffering in the conduct
of hostilities must appear to us to have been unnecessarily
increased by many of the actions of Germany; and, after
every possible allowance has been made, it must be admitted
that not a few of her actions have put back the customs
of humanity in warlike operations by more than five hundred
years. Some of these methods may possibly have an effect
upon our maritime communications in the near future, and
therefore the subject will repay a brief study.

Invention in the end has been a great benefactor of humanity,
but often in its first stages it entails suffering. Nature seems
to deliver up her secrets reluctantly and at the peril of those
who try to wrest them from her. The tale of inventors who
have been killed or maimed by their discoveries is long, but it
is a new and somewhat disquieting feature that the device of
the submarine has been directed to taking toll of innocent lives.
This is utterly repugnant to the custom of the sea in the building
up of which our nation has borne the larger part during almost
a thousand years. Thus an old treaty of Edward I maintains
the ideal of taking surety and giving safeguards for the wardship
of peace, right and equity amongst all manner of peoples
frequenting the seas named in the document[1]. That tradition
has developed till it reached the picture of the perfect seaman
given by the poet Spenser:

> Then which none more upright,
> Ne more sincere in word and deed profest;
> Moste voide of guile, most free from fowle despight,
> Doing himselfe and teaching others to doe right[2].

The law of the sea, namely to keep harmless women and
children; and, in time of war, merchant sailors also, has been
broken with tragic frequency in the undersea campaign of

---

[1] Possibly the original is worth quoting: "De seurté prendre & savegarde
doner en tous cas que mestier serra, & par ordinance de tous autres faits
necessaries a la garde des pees, droiture & equite entre toute manere des
gentz taunt d'autre seignurie come leur propre par illeque's passanz."
Printed in *Mare Clausum*, 1635, p. 276.

[2] Spenser, *The Faerie Queene*, IV. 6, xviii.

Germany. And one cannot help wondering if Kipling writes a new "Song of the English" will he still sing:

> We must feed our sea for a thousand years,
>   For that is our doom and pride,
> As it was when they sailed with the *Golden Hind*,
>   Or the wreck that struck last tide—
> Or the wreck that lies on the spouting reef
>   Where the ghastly blue-lights flare.
> If blood be the price of admiralty,
> If blood be the price of admiralty,
> If blood be the price of admiralty,
>   Lord God, we ha' bought it fair!

But is submarine ruthlessness, added to other perils of the sea, a "fair price"? Our whole experience—older than ocean travel and extending over all the oceans of the world—answers that it is not. There is something humanising in the spirit of wide waters which has established the convention of saving life at sea, a convention—if it may be so named—which has become so firmly fixed amongst our seafaring people that it scarcely needs to be spoken. The German submarine policy—however much allowance may be made for the callous irresponsibility of nerve-shaken individual commanders—shows an inability to recognise the whole spirit of the customs of the sea, which gives rise to several grave reflections. And these thoughts are serious, not only from the point of view of material damage, but from that of the spiritual principle. Even were the material damage much greater than it has been or is likely to be, that would be of infinitely less importance to a maritime power, such as we are, than the explicit disregard of this fundamental principle.

As a matter of fact our forefathers suffered and overcame worse things than we are likely to experience, as may be seen from an investigation of the losses of shipping during the Napoleonic wars. That enquiry is not an easy one, for there are unfortunately several gaps in the statistics, but sufficient data can be collected to present a general picture of the effect of those struggles on our shipping. Usually the situation is regarded from its final result which left us with more ships than at the beginning, but the stages by which that result was arrived at are not without a lesson, and perhaps some comfort[1].

It may be premised that in 1792 the number of ships owned by Great Britain, the adjacent islands and the Colonies was 16,079, with a tonnage of 1,540,145 or an average of 96 tons per ship[2]. By 1803 the number of ships had increased to 20,893, the tonnage to 2,167,863, giving an average of 104 tons per ship[3]. It is an interesting and instructive coincidence that in 1913—after 110 years—the number of ships belonging to the United Kingdom and registered under the Merchant Shipping Act of 1894 was almost exactly the same, being 20,938, while the gross tonnage had increased very greatly giving an average of 932 tons per vessel[4]. This figure of approximately 21,000, as representing the number of ships of Great Britain and the Colonies in 1803 and the number of ships of the United Kingdom in 1913, is worth remembering, since it affords a convenient basis of comparison of losses at the two periods.

During the Napoleonic wars the Government of the time was not communicative concerning British losses of shipping, and the position has been obscured by the record of history having contented itself with the final result, thereby omitting what is important at present, namely the processes by which that result was attained. As is well known, the end of the Napoleonic wars left our mercantile marine stronger than it had been in 1803 or at any previous date. But much had to

---

[1] As far as the existing position is concerned due allowance must be made for the increased importance of shipping, both for military and other vital needs. The final cure for the submarine menace is the technical one of the capture or destruction of hostile undersea craft, but until that is attained with certainty, it is practical wisdom, both from the standpoint of the present and the future, to build at least enough shipping to make good the losses.

[2] G. Chalmers, *An Estimate of the Comparative Strength of Great Britain*, 1794, p. 285.

[3] G. R. Porter, *Progress of the Nation*, 1838, Sections III. and IV. p. 171.

[4] *Statistical Abstract*, 1914, p. 300.

be done and suffered before this consummation was reached. It is often supposed that we gained by ships captured from the French; but, as a matter of fact, the balance of captures was very much against us. The French took no less than twelve times as many British ships as we succeeded in seizing French vessels. It is true that many American prizes were secured, but not nearly enough to make good our losses to the French. It is almost paradoxical that naval strength means large shipping losses, since the Power which can keep the sea risks its vessels, as distinguished from the enemy which is compelled to confine much of its mercantile marine to its ports. Also the usual casualties to ships continued, indeed the percentage was rather higher owing to the greater risks of ordinary navigation during hostilities.

For these and other reasons the position of British mercantile shipping during the first fifteen years of the nineteenth century was one of extraordinary interest, and it is necessary to investigate how it happened that, in spite of losses by war and shipwreck, it increased by the end of the war. The absence of complete records of the state of British shipping makes it desirable to devise a method of estimating the total losses and the means taken to meet them. There are fairly complete returns of the total registered shipping each year and also of the prize ships remaining on the register, while there are particulars of the amount of new construction. Data as to vessels purchased from foreigners or sold to foreigners do not appear to be available. If then we start with the registered tonnage in 1803 and add to that the amount of vessels built up to 1814 and that of prize ships, we should arrive at the total available tonnage at the later date. But we have the tonnage in 1814; and, accordingly, if that be deducted from the first total, the remainder will represent a fairly close estimate of the shipping lost through all causes during the twelve years. In that period the reduction in tonnage, calculated in this way, was over 40 per cent. or an average of about 4 per cent. per annum[1]. Indeed it may well

---

[1] See Appendix for the details.

have happened that, during those eventful twelve years, we lost one-half the shipping which we owned at the beginning. Moreover the losses were not evenly distributed. In 1810 they reached the maximum as far as has been recorded, the prizes taken by the French in that year having exceeded the average of the whole period by 50 per cent. and being double that of some years in it. Further, at the beginning the total amount of tonnage actually declined. It was 2,269,000 in 1804, and it had fallen to 2,264,000 tons in 1806. Gradually new construction began to make good losses of all kinds, and it was only in this way that the final satisfactory position was reached. This result was not attained at once. At first construction declined. In 1804 it was 70 per cent. of the average of the two previous years, and it fell by successive steps till 1808 when the total was only 42 per cent. of that of 1802–3. Afterwards there was an improvement. By 1811 it was nearly normal, and it became quite normal in 1815. The total amount of new building amounted to more than one-half of all the tonnage of 1803, and it is not too much to say that it was the strenuous and unremitting activities of our shipyards which saved the situation. Without such extreme application Great Britain would have emerged from the war with its shipping seriously, and even dangerously, depleted.

After the lapse of a century shipping has become much more important to all maritime countries, and the tragedy of the situation for the whole world, which has arisen through German piracy, is that the destruction, instead of the capture of mercantile vessels, may leave the world's stock of shipping very greatly reduced. The degree of construction will depend upon the extent to which the world's shipyards, as a whole, can repair losses while the war is actually in progress. It is one of the ironies of the position, that Germany, which is responsible for the scarcity by the inhumanity of its submarine and mining operations, is the only Power from which large actual captures of shipping have been made. Up to December, 1916, Captain Schröder estimated that 13·4 per cent. of its mercantile marine had been taken and was then being used by the Allies[1]. To this has to be added the seizure of vessels which had been interned in ports of the United States, which amounted to a further 10 per cent., making altogether a loss of approximately 25 per cent., or considerably more than one million tons. This loss to Germany represents only ships actually transferred or in process of being transferred to the carrying trade of its enemies. Ships in ports of some other countries, originally neutral, have been taken over or are likely to be taken over, and in addition there has not been included those vessels which have been sunk, or those interned in the ports of the remaining neutral countries, the fate of some of which appears to be subject to considerable doubt.

War is necessarily a transitory condition, but it is inevitable that the present struggle contains the seeds of much which will influence economic development in the future, perhaps even for generations to come. And this will be particularly applicable to shipping. Our conception of the position of Greater Britain and its communications with the rest of the world has remained too long in embryo. It is scarcely yet an explicit thought; indeed, to adopt the terminology of Kant, it is not even a category but the mere schematism of a category. Is it possible to give it reality from the economic point of view, when account is taken of possible changes in the near future? I think that to some extent this may be accomplished, though imperfectly.

The whole idea of a maritime State differs in its essentials from that of a land Power. The main gate of England does not face the Continent of Europe but is a water gate opening to the Atlantic. Our great concern is not with territory but with ocean routes for trade. The protection of these is the fundamental consideration in the defence of Greater Britain. Thus the oracle the Athenians found so hard to interpret, namely that ships are the only impregnable defence[2], still remains true. The maritime State differs from the land Power in so far as the centre of gravity of the latter remains relatively

---

[1] From the report of Schröder's paper in the *Maasbode* of Rotterdam, Dec. 29, 1916.

[2] Herodotus, VII. 141.

fixed, whereas that of the former shifts with the ceaseless change of the element from which it derives its whole vitality.

Communication by sea is the life-nerve of the existence of the British race in its present geographical distribution. It is only in this way that various members of the great family can specialise in the kind of production for which their country fits them by exchanging these with the others and with the rest of the world. The extent to which Great Britain has depended upon imported food is a commonplace, while the Dominions depend no less upon outside markets for the sale of the commodities which they chiefly produce. The main reason that transport by sea has been sought throughout history is its cheapness in comparison with that by land[1]. Ports are required partly for coaling partly for safety, and a hinterland behind the ports for the industrious population which supplies and consumes the goods which are conveyed by the ocean routes. It appears to be a German gloss upon history that the most bitter and most protracted struggles during more than two thousand years have always raged round coast-lines and harbours[2]. There is a deeper wisdom in Bacon's remark that "it was not the Romans that spread upon the world, but it was the world that spread upon the Romans: and that was the true way of greatness[3]."

What railways and canals are to inland states, secure ocean routes are to Greater Britain and its Possessions. They are the essential arteries by which its life-blood circulates. It follows that shipping may add to the wealth of a land Power, but is not essential to it: whereas to the maritime State it constitutes the necessary link that unites the parts together; as it has been finely said, ships are

Swift shuttles of an Empire's loom that weave us, main to main.

The provision of shipping is of special importance to a country whose destiny is upon the sea. It must have an effective

---

[1] Mahan, *The Influence of Sea-Power upon History*, 1660–1783, p. 15.
[2] Von Bülow, *Imperial Germany* (Eng. Trans. 1914), p. 25.
[3] Bacon, *Essays, On Plantations*.

control of the instruments upon which its internal communications depend. Even Adam Smith gave an approval, which was only slightly qualified, to the Navigation Acts, describing them as being "as wise as if they had been dictated by the most deliberate wisdom[1]." This passage is too often quoted apart from its context and an understanding of what it implies. Adam Smith wrote of these Acts in view of the naval position of Holland in the second half of the seventeenth century, which he thought was then "the only naval power which could endanger the safety of England." Accordingly, the degree of approval which he gives to these measures (and by inference to other restrictions designed for the same object) is conditioned by there being, at the time they are enforced or continued, a foreign naval Power sufficiently great to prejudice the security of Great Britain and the Colonies. In the near future it would appear that it would suffice if British-owned shipping maintained a somewhat similar proportion to that of the remainder of the world which it occupied in the years before the war. It may indeed be necessary that this proportion should be improved upon, since inter-Imperial communication leaves much to be desired. Strictly speaking that communication, regarded from the economico-political point of view, resembles a coasting trade—it is between two British ports, however widely separated they may be—and there can be no better form of national development than to improve it by judicious measures. Closely connected with this problem is the manning of the ships. Long before the war there was a movement for British sailors in British ships. If this meant what the words imply, namely, the employment of sailors born in Great Britain only, it was too narrow. In 1913 88·7 per cent. of the total seamen were British subjects, and 11·3 per cent. foreigners, while the percentage of the latter tends on the whole to decline[2]. It would appear that, apart from certain special services, such as that of pilots, the proportion of foreigners gives little ground for anxiety. But, considering the importance of the seaman in

---

[1] A. Smith, *Wealth of Nations* (ed. Cannan), I. p. 428.
[2] *Statistical Abstract*, 1914, p. 303.

the organisation of the British States and his essential function in their interconnection, his status should be improved. By the exigencies of ocean voyages, a large part of the seafaring population is debarred from exercising the important function of citizenship in voting for members of Parliament. It is a serious defect that an interest, upon which so much depends, should be able to record its suffrages only with irregularity. Though some changes in method would be necessary, it should be possible to devise a scheme by which opportunities would be given to the great majority of sailors to record their votes probably upon a special franchise suited to them. The delay which would be involved would not be very greatly in excess of that which occurs in completing an election in the constituency of Orkney and Shetland. In particular if the time comes when there will be some representative body for the British Empire, the men who control the essential mechanism which connects the parts should have an opportunity of making their voice heard in the determination of the policy of the whole.

Adequate shipping requires sufficient naval force for its defence. Even in time of peace, the seas must be policed, in order to prevent wrong and injury being done. Piracy and slave trading soon show sporadic attempts to recommence, if control is withdrawn. That the seas have become safe for international commerce is a great, but almost unrecognised, work of the navies of the maritime Powers and in a high degree of that of Great Britain. Thus there has grown up what may be called for the sake of brevity the modern custom of the sea; and, in my view, it has been one of the greatest errors of Germany that this has been violated by the inhumanity of her submarine operations and the policy of indiscriminate minelaying. Unless there can be guarantees against the recurrence of this, it will mean the loss of much progress made in the past towards maintaining safety of life at sea; since, even in time of peace, the implied menace would still remain. The better minds amongst seamen in the modern world have had a deep and almost religious sense of the high purpose of their calling.

For instance Camoëns makes Vasco da Gama pray in the following terms:

> Be now the saviour God,
> Safe in thy care, what dangers have we past!
> And shalt thou leave us, leave us now at last
> To perish here—our dangers and our toils
> To spread thy laws[1].

Raleigh concludes his *Observations upon the Navy and Sea Service* with the words: "for well we know, that God worketh all things here among us mediately by a secondary means, the which means of our defence and safety being shipping and sea forces are to be esteemed as His gifts and then only available and beneficial when He withal vouchsafeth His Grace to use them aright[2]." In a more concise form one of Nelson's commanders expressed his ideal to be inflexibly just in order to be effectively humane[3].

Justice and humanity have been the main characteristics of the great seafaring nations, and these must remain the essence of the development of oversea communications. It is these that have made the freedom of the seas and only by these can the freedom of the seas be maintained. And from this there follows that security of sea-borne commerce which maritime nations require.

The circumstances of the British peoples, as a maritime State, have involved for the sake of their trade a preponderance in shipping and therefore adequate sea power to protect that shipping. It is for the world to judge whether the law of the sea, by which Great Britain bound herself and which she enforced, is more conducive to civilisation and progress than that which Germany proposes to substitute for it.

The present war might almost be said to have added a third dimension to hostilities. Prior to the twentieth century

---

[1] *The Lusiad*, Book VII. (Mickle's Translation), cf. *Roteiro da Viagem fez Dom. Vasco da Gama em* 1497, 1838, pp. 1, 41.

[2] Raleigh, *Works*, 1751, II. p. 107.

[3] Sir Alexander Ball, Governor of Malta. Coleridge, *The Friend*, 3rd Landing Stage, Essay 3.

battles were confined, with a few minor exceptions, to the surface of the earth and of the sea. Now they have been extended from the horizontal to the vertical plane by the new engines of air-craft and submarines. Both have an effect upon communications. As far as the experience of this war has shown, even when the submarine has been used as by Germany, it has an effect in the temporary interruption of shipping; but it appears to conform to Mahan's description of the ultimate futility of commerce destroying[1], since it has not sufficed to liberate Germany's ocean trade, that having ceased for all practical purposes since the war began. There is the converse side in the relation of air-craft to communications by land. In the latter case it would seem that, in at least one respect, the aeroplane has an advantage over the submarine. It is usual to speak of ocean routes, but, in an open sea, the course from one port to another can be varied, if necessary. A successful attack by a submarine has no effect in impairing the route itself—to bomb the sea is useless—but a successful attack upon land communications has relatively permanent results. Damage to bridges or the permanent way of a railway will require time for repair. Traffic by sea is almost indefinitely flexible. It is like some of the enchantments in old romances, where however the body, which is protected by magic, is wounded the hurts close themselves immediately. But the injury inflicted upon land communications requires time to be repaired, and alternative routes are often fully used already. Thus, on the whole, it may be conjectured that the balance of invention is not unfavourable to the defence of marine transport, and it might even have tended to be favourable if the dictates of humanity in war (which it was believed were firmly established) had been observed.

These are highly technical points which fall largely, though not altogether, outside the scope of the present discussion. But they have an intimate connection with a related topic without some reference to which the reasoning would be incomplete. Warfare, as has been shown, has extended into the

---

[1] Mahan, *The Influence of Sea-Power upon History*, 1660–1783, p. 329.

third dimension. Is it possible that commerce may ultimately do the same; and, if that should happen, what would be the effect upon the communications of Greater Britain? This cannot be described as an altogether speculative proposition, since before the war a company had been formed in Germany for the carrying of passengers by air-ships, and during the war a few spectacular voyages were made by cargo-carrying submarines between Germany and the United States.

On the supposition that in the future submarines might be employed to carry cargo to a considerable extent, it seems probable that such a development would not produce any marked effect upon intercommunication between Great Britain, the Dominions and Possessions. The submersibles would require ports and loading and unloading facilities not very dissimilar from the present day cargo vessel; if anything, secure and well-equipped harbours would be more rather than less necessary. Accordingly, the advantage which the British Empire enjoys in its fuel stations would certainly not be diminished; and therefore, if this change came, it would lead to no disturbance in the communications of Greater Britain. As to its probability, apart from some limited special use which might be discovered for submersible craft, they do not appear likely to be of importance in commerce. At present they have an advantage for purposes of war (which may or may not be permanent) in that they can escape detection when occasion requires it. The future course of invention cannot be predicted, but, as far as available information extends, it is evident that in the more immediate future the cost of carrying freight by submersible would be prohibitive.

It has already been shown that the invention of aerial navigation has given a maritime Power advantages as regards communications over one whose strength is on land. Should air-ships be adapted to commercial purposes, the balance of advantage would be in part reversed. Assuming that passengers are carried, and that foreign Powers would give facilities for landing for the supply of petrol, the advantage of ports would be to some extent neutralised. Access to the sea would no longer be as important as it is at present. Should this development come, it would in all probability apply first to urgent passenger traffic, since a very great saving in time could be effected. This would have an important effect upon the representative and administrative organising of the consolidation of Greater Britain. For purposes of government, distance is measured more by the time consumed in travelling from place to place than by actual mileage, and therefore so great an increase in the speed of transit would bring the Dominions and Possessions nearer to Great Britain, and would remove many difficulties in the smooth working of a representative system. An Imperial Aerial mail might bring the towns of eastern Canada as near London, in terms of time, as the north of Scotland was before the war. Necessarily other places would be similarly brought closer, but the reduction in the time spent in travel would confer the largest relative advantage on the more distant places to which it was applicable. The conveyance of goods by air as yet belongs to the province of the writer of scientific romances. But who can say with confidence that it is impossible? In any case such a change is not likely to come quickly; and, even should it take place eventually, much will have happened in the meantime. The distribution of population may have changed as between different parts of the Empire, and some of the Dominions, now called new countries, will be on the way to become old countries. Trade routes would not be greatly changed, though the density with which they were used would possibly be different. Even assuming that considerable freight were diverted from the sea to the air, nothing much would happen beyond the smoothing out of some of the routes in places to make them straighter. Granting that our ports would be less essential—being now used by that traffic still carried by sea—the geographical dispersion of British territory might be expected to suffice, at least in part and perhaps altogether, to make good the loss of traffic at the existing ports. It would be favourably situated to tap many of the important new routes. Where there was a long stretch of ocean to be traversed conditions would remain much the same, except where the ocean route greatly diverges from a straight line owing to the configuration of the land. On the other side, where there is a sea route and an overland route, it would not follow that the air course would follow the shortest straight line over the land. Possibly the same conditions—which account for the irregularities in railway maps, namely the collection of traffic—would compel the new service to descend at those places (or some of them) where goods are at present collected for transportation.

Looking back over the history of invention during the last quarter of a century, and taking account of the acceleration that may follow this war, many and surprising discoveries may be anticipated. The nature of these cannot of course be fore-casted; but, judging by the possible application of some which have been considered as hypothetical, while there will be gains and losses, there is nothing in what can be guessed concerning future developments, even of a revolutionary character, in communication which need occasion serious anxiety. Rather, given energy and determination, a continuance of success in overseas trade may be expected.

While these considerations are necessarily highly speculative, no apology need be made for discussing them. The Greeks had a saying that the best prophet was he who guessed rightly[1], and peace treaties and reconstruction involve the looking ahead for a period so great that we can do little more than guess. But it is at least something to guess not ignobly, when the future of an Empire is concerned. On the material side in a maritime State such as that which unites Great Britain with the Britons beyond the seas, there are few things more important than shipping, the indispensable mechanism of intercommunication. The nature of that State has given us a place of importance upon the seas; but its greatness, both in peace and war, will depend upon the "inflexible justice" with which it is used. This thought has been the golden thread that runs through the best of our naval history, and it grows as time goes on. It is

[1] Μάντις δ' ἄριστος ὅστις εἰκάζει καλῶς.

this which, in the end, will be our most powerful plea at the bar of history, when our case is tried. If, when the full tale is told, it will appear that British sea power made for the progress of civilisation, then as a nation we may claim to have offered something, not wholly unworthy, towards the progress of humanity.

The extent and the limits of this idea present extraordinary practical difficulties when it comes into contact with that of the defence of our commerce and internal communications between the parts of Greater Britain. In time of peace the minimum of restraint is likely, on the whole, to accord most with both ideals. No doubt there are difficulties now and difficulties will remain in the future, but the conception of inter-Imperial voyages as being of the nature of purely internal communications of Greater Britain affords a distinction which may be of practical use. Apart from this, the general conclusion of this enquiry leads to a result similar to that in the previous lecture, namely that, after the necessary provision is made for defence of our commerce, the maximum amount of liberty is in agreement with the principle of justice. It is thus, and as far as can be seen thus only, that we can be effectively humane to all who would use the sea and seek the hospitality of our ports for any legitimate purpose.

THE SURPRISES OF PEACE

Quo teneam vultus mutantem Protea nodo?

HORACE.

THE SURPRISES OF PEACE

Bacon in one of his Essays speaks of innovations as "the births of time," and it cannot be questioned that the peace which will follow the present upheaval of the nations will constitute a new epoch in history. The time of war and trial has been fruitful in surprises, many of which were disagreeable. As far as can be judged from the apparent changes of plan by the military authorities of the chief countries involved in hostilities, war produced many situations and problems which had not been anticipated by those who had made it their life-long study. Certainly, in commerce and industry, all those who have studied the changes of the past three years will be candid enough to confess that their expectations have often been falsified by events. Nor is this limitation of the practical judgment a matter to occasion wonder when the circumstances are understood. Rather, the surprising fact has been, not that commercial and financial calculation has been so fallible; but, in the unprecedented circumstances, that it was not much more fallible. Experience in business is largely personal, and therefore its more immediate influence is limited to the space of one or two generations. It is true that in the past it has been our fate to take part in many great wars, but it is a matter of doubt to what extent war-time commerce in previous campaigns resembled that which is carried on at present. Even in the last hundred years the mechanism of commerce has been transformed. Not only has the world been drawn closer together, but the ramifications of credit have been enormously extended. Diplomatists talk of world power, but there was the fact of a world commerce in which all the chief producing countries appeared to be inextricably interwoven by reason of mutual dependence and mutual engagements. The comparative isolation of the Central Powers was an event which seemed in advance to have been impossible without the rending asunder of the whole fabric of commercial relations. And if the attempt is made to return in imagination to the world as it appeared in 1913, it is not remarkable that there were some who held that the intricacy of international commerce would make a long-continued war impossible. Yet our present experience shows that, though there was great dislocation, trade has been able to flow in some of the old channels and even to open up new ones in the attempt to meet the demands of war. In fact the recuperative power of British industry has been proved by the course of events, as far as it has yet revealed itself, to have been very greatly underestimated.

Modern commerce finds its supreme expression in the anticipation of the future. The application of science to industry tends to lengthen the time of production, while on the other side what is produced is usually both greater in volume and more efficient in character. The protraction of that production which seeks a world market makes the forecasting of the demand, which is not yet in existence, a necessity in almost all important industries. The producer must create from within his own mind the vision of those conditions with which he is concerned as they will be, not merely in the future but at a fixed date in that future. It is necessary for him to divine how forces, which he cannot control, will behave, and at the same time he must co-ordinate with these forces other causes the action of which he can direct to a greater or less extent. Stated in this abstract form, the practical problem seems to be one of remarkable difficulty; but, in normal circumstances, it is accomplished with sufficient general precision. The task of the producer is facilitated by the continuity of events, where the changes which happen are regular, and move in certain directions which can be estimated. Many conditions which exert great weight in the ultimate effect remain relatively unchanged; and in normal circumstances, these may be neglected in framing forecasts. But in the abnormal state of war all this is changed. Not only do new and highly uncertain phenomena emerge with disconcerting suddenness, but the causal values of old conditions change. And the function of judging and laying plans for the future is rendered more difficult by the fact that, despite the somewhat vociferous claims of "scientific management," the higher forms of commercial skill have remained essentially an art, and thus the process is largely instinctive, as it is almost inarticulate. Those who are most successful can rarely explain the thought-processes by which their conclusions have been reached, indeed it sometimes happens that their own account of the reasons which have prompted their actions represents not those that in reality determined them, but merely such as chanced to remain in their memory when the course of their mental activity came to be reviewed in reflection. There, as in other instances of what is sometimes called the "creative imagination," the thinker becomes absorbed in that which his mind is fashioning, and the stages of progress towards a final practical result become merged in the actual end to be attained. It follows that this submerged character of much of the planning of practical life makes it exceedingly difficult to incorporate important new conditions in the forecast and at the same time to give due weight to the altered values of those old conditions which survive. In such circumstances, particularly if hostilities come without warning, the first result is a feeling of consternation. What happened in 1793 was described in graphic terms by Sir Francis Baring, the founder of the famous house of Baring Brothers. "A circumstance," he wrote, "which very materially contributed to produce the distress of 1793 was the sudden, unexpected declaration of war. That dreadful calamity is usually preceded by some indication which enables the commercial community to make preparation. On this occasion the short notice rendered the least degree of general preparation impossible[1]." But the financiers and traders of the last half of the eighteenth century were far from being unacquainted with war; whereas at the beginning of the twentieth century there had been little experience of any but very minor contests.

[1] Tooke rather disputes the effect of the war in contributing to the discredit of the period. *History of Prices*, I. p. 177.

Accordingly, the shock and the disturbance of the summer of 1914 were all the greater, and enterprise was at first stunned.

Gradually and, at first, very tentatively, business began to adapt itself to the new and strange conditions. The very state of hostilities which had dislocated commerce forced it to resume by the insistent demand for naval and military supplies of all kinds. Just because we are living with war-industry around us, and because changes have come gradually, these are liable to escape attention in the midst of the exceedingly grave preoccupations of the time. One of these characteristics of commerce in war time is the limitation of prevision. The control of industry in the interests of diplomatic and military exigencies, uncertainties of supplies of materials and difficulties in obtaining labour, the new risks of communications overseas, the fluctuations of military success in various theatres of war, all unite in making any estimates of the future hazardous in the extreme. Also there are influences which are mainly psychological. The general attitude of the mercantile community in the early months of war had an important influence upon the scale of production during the first stage of hostilities. In the sixteenth and seventeenth centuries there was a prevalent opinion (which was probably erroneous) that commerce prospered during war. Hence there was enterprise and confidence, with the frequent result that the ill-developed credit system of those times was unable to bear the double strain of financing war-expenditure and supporting an active state of industry, with the result that crises ensued[1]. In 1914 the unexpected declaration of war, the strangeness and the dread of hostilities upon so large a scale and the almost complete absence of data conduced to the contrary consequence, and at the beginning of the present struggle production was severely curtailed. The majority of those directing industry contented themselves at that stage by waiting upon events instead of attempting to anticipate and control them. The great risks of so great a war under modern conditions in its effects upon commerce were felt so strongly that they tended to crush initiative.

[1] Scott, *Joint Stock Companies*, I. pp. 464–470.

The attitude of mind which I have endeavoured to interpret was only a first stage though an important one. Towards the end of 1914, or at least early in 1915, it was succeeded by a new phase. Some of the most serious risks of the first weeks of war (such as a breakdown of credit or a general interruption of ocean trade) seemed to have disappeared. The circulation of money, disbursed by the Government, began to act as a stimulant to trade, and a number of industries became active. Such activity however was not normal. It was confined to a group of trades, such as those contracting for the Government, and later to others which experienced an improved demand through the increase of wages in munition areas. At this time there was a second danger-point, namely the risk of speculation in commodities. Shortage and interruption of supply with rising prices tended towards a disposition to accumulate stocks, but this was checked by the intervention of the State, on the one side by a gradual and growing control of markets and on the other by the institution of excess profits duty. In principle, widespread diversions both of demand and supply have caused temporary monopolies of stocks of certain goods, while there has also been something of a monopoly in several kinds of skill and specialised ability. In such cases, especially in periods of national crisis, it is desirable that the Government should regulate the supply of stocks and services where war has created unexpected monopolistic advantages for individuals. That regulation again acted as a distinct check upon the nascent speculative activity. Further, the combined difficulties of obtaining labour and raw materials compelled very many manufacturers to restrict themselves to short views, and they were forced to content themselves with attempting merely "to carry on," rather than to frame large plans for the future.

External influences co-operated with purely mental qualities in limiting and restraining anticipations of the future. The chances of war, the fluctuations of campaigns extending over such a wide area, the personal anxieties arising out of the dangers of relatives in the Army, all together exerted an influence upon the faculty of judgment. Nervous strain inevitably, though insensibly, checks the imaginative faculty, at least amongst a northern race. This is not a necessary consequence, sometimes it is found to induce an extreme mental activity in which there is an element of fever and excitement. There is over-stimulation, and the poise of the judgment is impaired. As far as this war has proceeded there are few signs of the latter characteristic. Generally speaking the broad effect upon commercial forecasts has been to emphasize the need of caution and a disposition to avoid the forming of extensive plans for the largely unknown conditions which will arise after the war. In this attitude of mind there appears to be an element of unconscious adaptation to our surroundings at the time. Stress of emotion—and it is only those who are either sub-human or super-human who can view the agony of civilisation without passion—inevitably influences the reason and imagination, even to the extent of playing havoc with the measuring of evidence[1]. Thus, although the inspiration of great events may be missed, it seems on the whole to be wiser to restrict anticipation. Commerce, industry, credit and finance for the time have been made subservient to the military art. It is as if they have been moved to quite a different plane from that upon which they had their being in time of peace. Thus the activity of mind in forecasting the future in the later stages of the war is not so much abnormal as sub-normal. Psychological and external conditions both tend to restrict it. No doubt it chafes against the restraint which it feels is checking its power; but it seems better, for the time, to recognise the limits which war creates, rather than, by ignoring these, to risk a catastrophe by neglecting all those difficulties, whether subjective or objective, which the circumstances of the time impose.

This analysis is only the starting-point for an approach to the main problem of the present lecture, namely how, with the data at present available, we are to regard the future of commerce when peace has been re-established. In this discussion there will be involved not only the forecasts of men of affairs,

---

[1] Venn, *Logic of Chance*, p. 65.

but the interest of the general community. For a nation whose trade was its very existence, there has been in the past a prevalent lack of attention to the state of industry and commerce. In the present century much thought and effort had been given to schemes of social betterment, and this was laudable. But when war is ended, the rapidity of recovery from its material losses will be very largely conditioned by the extension and success of commerce. Since every citizen will be affected personally by the rate at which that recovery takes place, the underlying condition in the future state of commerce will be of surpassing interest and importance to him. It follows that industrial and commercial conditions in the first years of peace deserve the most careful consideration. But the forecasting of the future is subject to quite exceptional difficulties. In 1916 and up to the spring of 1917 activity of mind in the making of well-judged anticipations may be described as sub-normal, partly for reasons already stated, partly too through other causes. The stress of the times has called many of those, who direct industry, to the performance of other tasks which are designed to aid the national cause, and consequently much thought and energy must be diverted to these special duties. Also, except perhaps in some of the specifically war industries, the assistance of all the younger men, who filled comparatively responsible positions, has been withdrawn. As a result, almost all the leadership has become concentrated in the hands of the middle aged or of those who are older. Hence something of the buoyancy and hopefulness of youth has been absent; and it may be doubted if the stimulus of a great national endeavour can wholly make good what is wanting.

Altogether apart from the subjective side, there are all the uncertainties which arise out of the situation itself. At any time the imagining of the future is difficult. Even in normal times the possibilities of error are great. These have been described in a somewhat different connection by Dr Venn in the following terms:—"Our conviction generally rests upon a sort of chaotic basis composed of an infinite number of inferences and analogies of every description, and these moreover distorted by our state of feeling at the time dimmed by the degree of our recollection of them afterwards, and probably revived from time to time with varying force according to the way in which they happen to combine at the moment. To borrow a striking illustration from Abraham Tucker, the superstructure of our convictions is not so much to be compared to the solid foundations of an ordinary building, as to the piles of the houses of Rotterdam which rest somehow in a deep bed of soft mud. They bear their weight securely enough, but it would not be easy to point out accurately the dependence of the different parts upon one another. Directly we begin to think of the amount of our belief, we have to think of the arguments by which it is produced—in fact, these arguments will intrude themselves without our choice. As each in turn flashes through the mind, it modifies the strength of our conviction; we are like a person listening to the confused hubbub of a crowd, where there is always something arbitrary in the particular sound which we choose to listen to[1]." If this be the case in ordinary times how much more difficult is the problem, when, to adapt the metaphor, we do not know whether the upheaval amongst the nations may not have caused the soft mud at the foundation to shift? Or when there is added to the noise of the crowd the concussion of great guns heard in the distance? There are few who have the power of abstraction and concentration which according to one account is attributed to Archimedes who is said to have been found by a Roman soldier so deeply immersed in a problem that he was not aware that Syracuse had been stormed[2]. Rather one notes as more human the tragic note in the postscript of a letter I received from a Belgian colleague during the German advance in 1914— "as I write," he said, "I hear the guns of the enemy—and they seem to be coming nearer."

It is clear that estimates of the future are beset with exceptional pitfalls. Indeed it almost seems that in the special circumstances prediction is useless. Yet there remains a certain sturdy optimism which refuses to be discomfited, and

---

[1] *Logic of Chance*, pp. 66, 67.   [2] Plutarch, *Life of Marcellus*.

anticipations, some of them not well informed, are being ventilated with enthusiasm, and often advanced by vigorous propaganda. It not infrequently happens either that those most acquainted with the circumstances offer no opinion or else, it may be, that two men with apparently equal opportunities of judging reach opposite conclusions as to the future. Thus there is the danger that schemes for reconstruction—to mention only one instance—may be initiated and developed by those who are unable to envisage possible future events in their true perspective. And there may be another danger also. What I have called the sub-normal power of anticipation will not last amongst the business community. When an Allied victory has been secured, the mainspring of hope and enterprise which has been pressed down for so long, will be released, and there will be a disposition to expect too much from the peace which will then be inaugurated. For many years, even before the war, Europe had been existing in the uneasy nightmare of excessive armaments. If, as is deeply to be hoped and as may be expected, it seems that the menace of militarism has been dispersed like an evil dream, there will be the beginnings of exceedingly confident expectations of what the future holds for commerce. Then the disposition may be to discount the coming years in too optimistic a spirit. A rebound from caution is always a possibility, with the risk of expecting too much with consequent disappointment.

It seems then that whether we wish it or not, even now, anticipations of the early years of peace must be made, indeed are being made; and it will not be out of place to enquire if either economic theory or past experience suggests anything that is likely to be helpful. It is perhaps easier to deal with the mental attitude involved, negatively rather than positively in the first instance. The natural disposition is to begin by framing schemes which are designed to remedy some pressing inconvenience which has impressed the popular imagination. This has always been a common aftermath of war, and it is a necessary element in reconstruction. Closely connected with it is the effort to restore former conditions which had been replaced by less desirable ones during the period of hostilities.   Here much will depend upon the method employed.   Piecemeal views are strongly to be deprecated.   Action in the first case may be unnecessary and even prejudicial, for the phenomena it is designed to remedy may be such as would not in any case survive the end of the period of transition from war to peace. Hence the efforts to remove them are not only largely wasted but they set up new conditions which in their turn lead to further effects.   Or, in the second case, it is desirable to ascertain, in the first instance, whether those conditions it is proposed to put in the place of others are the best in the new circumstances. It is far from being obvious that methods which were best in 1914 will be equally satisfactory in the first year of peace. What appears to be required is a serious attempt to envisage social conditions or commerce, as the case may be, with a wide and comprehensive outlook in order to discern as far as possible what of former practices should be retained and what should be replaced by something new and better.

Further as a nation we are largely dominated by phrases. What are called principles are often no more than catchwords. They may represent a point of view as long as the circumstances to which they are applied remain fairly stable, though even there the living reality will often be found to have outgrown the formula which expressed it more or less accurately at an earlier stage.   But in all those countries over which the tornado of war has passed, the things themselves will in many cases have suffered great changes, and the old principles, which were already little more than catchwords, will no longer apply. It is once more the wasteful effort to pour new wine into the old bottles, when the owner of the latter will probably blame the potency of the liquid and not his own false economy. There is a fable of Julius C. Hare which exactly illustrates this point.   "Once upon a time," he tells us, "there was a certain country, in which from local reasons, the land could be divided in no way so conveniently as into four-sided figures. A mathematician, having remarked this, ascertained the laws of all such figures, and laid them down fully and accurately.   His countrymen learnt to esteem him a philosopher; and his precepts were observed religiously for years. A convulsion of nature at length changed the face and local character of the district: whereupon a skilful surveyor, being employed to lay out some fields afresh, ventured to give one of them five sides. The innovation is talkt of universally, and is half applauded by some younger and bolder members of the community: but a big mouthed and weighty doctor, to set the matter at rest forever, quotes the authority of the above mentioned mathematician, *that fixer of agricultural positions, and grand landmark of posterity*, who has demonstrated to the weakest apprehensions that a field ought never to have more than four sides: and then he proves to the satisfaction of all his hearers, that a pentagon has more[1]." Here, difficult as it will be, the only safeguard will be a resolute search for the facts and a deliberate and at the same time a fairly expeditious facing of the facts, when discovered. For it is to be remembered that the resumption of civil life in all its manifold activities will not wait on the niceties of economic classification and ratiocination, as it was carried on in the past. While examination of facts should be thorough, to be of use, it must at the same time be rapid. The task is enormous; and, when it is remembered how difficult the general public found it to face the realities of the situation in the midst of times of crisis during hostilities, not more than a modified success can be anticipated when everything seems fair and promising after peace has been concluded.

Reliance upon former principles is the resource of one type of mind—that which is commonly called conservative, and which in reality overestimates the importance of continuity. There is the opposed attitude, which seeks and is stimulated by variety. The latter type is liable to overestimate the magnitude of the changes which will have been effected by the war and its consequences. To it all things will seem to be new; and it will be eager to try new methods. Here again there will be waste of effort, since, implicitly, continuity is denied; and former experience is regarded as so much lumber. But experience

[1] *Guesses at Truth* (1873), p. 94.

is valuable, if rightly used—the problem will be to discover how far it is applicable to the new circumstances. In fine, from this point of view, there will be a double problem—on the one side to trace continuity with the past; and, on the other to recognise and to give due weight to the changes which will be inevitable.

Further it is not to be expected that the war-organisation which has been developed during the last two years can be replaced immediately by the new peace-organisation which will succeed it eventually. Rather, there must be a period of transition. The mere signing of a peace treaty cannot of itself at once recreate the normal mechanism of ordinary industrial life. Demobilisation alone will take time. Also the restoration of the accustomed channels in which commerce was wont to flow, or the discovery of new channels, cannot be effected without some delay. At this stage it will be necessary, though difficult, to believe that it is transitory, not permanent. And yet it will be impossible to wait until the final, normal, industrial life has been re-established. Here the element of time in all practical forecasts is of outstanding importance. It is not only necessary to frame a moderately accurate forecast of conditions that are to come. As has been finely said, the best practical minds "should have ears to hear the distant rustling of the wings of Time. Most people only catch sight of it as it is flying away. When it is overhead, it darkens their view[1]." But more than this, the valuable estimate is not that which will prove right at some time, but which is fulfilled at a time that has been fixed in advance. It must predict what will happen, not in an undetermined future, but in one a certain number of months ahead.

Calculation where the conditions will be so fluctuating and so uncertain seems to exist only in the form of "a licensed irregularity." Prices, credit, currency, labour and tariffs all together make a kaleidoscope of apparently baffling changes. Yet beneath all the mutability there will be a nexus of fixity. This is to be sought less in external conditions than in the

[1] *Guesses at Truth*, p. 416.

broad facts of human nature. In other words, those things that are connected with immaterial wealth may be expected to be relatively more predictable than other conditions which are more material. Not that the two can be disconnected except in analysis, since, rather, the former is the foundation of the latter. Much has been said and written of the materialism of life in the opening years of the present century, and yet it has been one of the paradoxes of recent months that, "while there never has been a war in which material appliances have been so important, at the same time, it is no less true that there never was one in which immaterial wealth, and even moral ideals, were so supreme[1]." And some estimate, even if only a tentative one, may be formed of the more probable developments of the immaterial characteristics which will influence social and economic changes in the first years of peace. The nation will have been roused from the lethargy into which it had fallen during the long years of commercial success of the Victorian era. It would be idle to believe that the experience of the severe test of war will leave the national character unaffected. Even more, when the epoch-making nature of the contest is kept in view—at once the final overthrow of mediaevalism and the last Crusade—will it be seen to be impossible that there should be any complete return to the pre-war outlook. There is more than a fragment of truth in the saying that "things are what we make them," and the process of fashioning them depends to no small extent upon the spirit in which we undertake the task. We can only discern dimly what it is probable that historians will emphasize, namely the majesty of thoughts and ideas which have mobilised the populations of more than half the world and at the same time have inspired them to face extreme hardships and horrors. How is it possible to imagine that after such an experience, the mental attitude of those who control and carry on commerce and industry will be what it was before? Old ways of thinking will have been changed; and, it may be, will have been transformed. There is a passage of deep significance in which Emerson expresses his conception

[1] Scott, "On Repairing the Waste of War" in *Scientia*, July, 1916.

of the English character. "The slow, deep English mass smoulders with fire, which at last sets all its borders in flame. The wrath of London has a long memory, and, in its hottest heat, a register and rule. Half their strength they put not forth. They are capable of a sublime resolution, and if hereafter the war of races, often predicted and making itself a war of opinions also (a question of despotism and liberty coming from Eastern Europe), should menace civilization, these sea-kings may take once more to their floating castles and find a new home and a second millennium of power in their Colonies[1]." Civilization has been menaced, but it has been the men of the Dominions who have came in their "sea castles " to aid in saving the liberties of Europe. What is truly striking in Emerson's tribute to the English character (and what is even truer of British character as a whole), is the amount of strength and force which is held in reserve save in times of crisis. It appears to resemble the secret reserve of some companies which is carefully concealed. It seems that it is impossible to use this hidden strength unless in an extreme emergency. The demands of war have forced the calling out of these reserved powers of character, mind and strength. Indeed it is not too much to say that the exigencies of the struggle have revealed them. When the emergency is over these powers will not sink back at once to their previous quiescence. Once set in motion, their activity will continue, though in all probability at a slowly diminishing rate. Reference has also been made to the anticipated acceleration of invention and improvements in commercial methods generally, which, as they come to fruition, will increase the productivity of industry.

These are all important elements in forecasting the character and dimensions of industry when it is resumed under a peace-organisation, and they are almost entirely favourable. But, at the same time, it must be fully recognised that there are also tendencies implicitly contained in the state of hostilities which may exercise an unfavourable influence, and to that extent would neutralise, and, it might even be, counterbalance those already

---

[1] *English Traits*, "Essay on Character."

described. The quickened mental apprehension which usually follows a great war cannot be confined to the removing of social and industrial functions which have survived their usefulness. It is at once critical and constructive. And the criticism is applied widely. Thus there is at least the danger that methods and institutions may be displaced in favour of others which prove in the end to be not better but worse. And so, while there is gain in the hastening of improvements and reforms which would otherwise have been long delayed; at the same time, there is all the wasted effort of the failures which result from overdriving the chariot of reform. That there will be such mistakes is inevitable; but, balancing gains against losses, it may be expected with a considerable degree of confidence that the final advantage will lie on the side of the former. This shows the remarkable contrast in the consequences of war upon material wealth and immaterial wealth respectively. The amount of positive destruction and the disorganisation of production make it probable that the best that can be expected is that, after the re-establishment of normal conditions, the total annual production of goods (that is, what is called " the real national income") will not be less than it was immediately before the war. In other words, all the increase in national wealth which would have taken place, if there had been no war, has been lost. On the other hand, there is at least a chance, indeed it might be said a fair degree of probability, that the growth of immaterial wealth of the kind just described will be accelerated and not checked by the fact that a war has taken place. If this be so, it may be expected that ultimately, though after some delay, this improvement will react in a favourable manner upon material wealth also.

It would be idle to ignore the comparatively serious risks of renewed disorganisation of commerce even after peace has been restored. It is exceedingly difficult to form an opinion as to what will be the final effect of the war upon credit. During hostilities confidence and the discounting of the future has been sub-normal. But when peace is in sight there is a possibility of a wave of optimism in business, which will demand more of the future than the existing conditions will admit. In this case it is possible that credit might be overstrained, and a crisis would result which would be followed by depression. Again, if that danger-point were safely passed, another would be reached a few years after peace had been concluded. At first people may act cautiously and exercise great discretion. Their expectations would be comparatively moderate, and these would be fulfilled. Gradually, as time went on, boldness would succeed caution, and the scale of enterprise would be extended rapidly. But soon there would be cause for alarm, since the scarcity of capital at that stage might easily precipitate a crisis. Much of the employment of capital in the first two or three years after peace must be in uses which will yield a very slow return, such as the building of houses or the making of the more durable instruments of production, as for instance, ships. New capital will be scarce in any case, and much of that which must be first employed after the war, will have brought in very small returns two or three years after peace. But if, at that time, many and extensive schemes have been launched, they will have pledged themselves, in effect, to raise capital which will not be available to the extent required, and this would impose a strain upon credit which it might not be able to bear.

Another possible cause of a dislocation of industry when the war is over would be the occurrence of widespread and protracted labour disputes. Since the labour position during the war has been far from clear, it is all the more difficult to speak of that which is likely to follow it. At the outbreak of war a number of important wages-disputes appeared to be imminent. These were dealt with, in the first instance, by the endeavour to postpone discussion during the conduct of hostilities. The length of time over which the war extended as well as other causes made it appear desirable to attempt to make some readjustments of rates of wages and occasionally of conditions of employment while the struggle still continued. Though there have been a number of disquieting incidents, on the whole a considerable degree of success has been attained, and this suggests a measure of hope for the future. We are perhaps a little too prone to regard friction in the fixing of wages as a phenomenon apart from others which co-exist with it. General conditions, as well as the attitude of mind of employers and employed are exceedingly important. During the war both sides should have begun to learn that there is a patriotism in daily work as well as in other types of national service. The need for this will not cease when the war ends, for larger and more efficient production will be required to help in making good some of the losses. Moreover the sharing in common dangers has united all classes of the community to a much greater extent than had been the case in recent years. To regard serious labour disputes as inevitable is a gloomy prognostication which in effect presupposes a permanent imperfection in the industrial system. Disputes involve colossal economic waste, and it is a question if the nation will be able to afford them. The question of confining causes of disputes and eventually perhaps removing them altogether, is one of the most serious problems with which the industry of the future is faced. Hitherto, perhaps, too much dependence has been placed on the mere mechanism of prevention and too little upon the attitude of the parties to each other. To borrow a metaphor from medicine, preventative rather than curative measures are required. If the chief causes of friction could be first isolated and later rendered innocuous much good would have been accomplished. If the new spirit of harmony and seriousness is rightly directed immediately upon the close of hostilities, the way would at least be prepared for further progress. After the orgy of strife which has devastated some of the fairest lands of Europe, there will follow a time of calm, which should be taken advantage of to the fullest extent in order to establish better relations at home in our industry as well as internationally. The war has given us what social reformers have longed for vainly during the last half-century, namely the opportunity of making a fresh start as far as that is possible. If we fail to take advantage of it, there will be a tragic waste of a chance which occurs only once in several generations.

Just two hundred years ago Nicholas Rowe—then poet
laureate—wrote two odes upon Peace.   While his verses leave
something to be desired as poetry, there is much in the senti-
ments which he expressed that fits the times upon which we may
soon hope to enter.

> Our passions, like the seasons, turn;
> And now we laugh, and now we mourn.
> Britannia late oppressed with dread,
> Hung her declining drooping head:
> A better visage now she wears,
> And now at once she quits her fears:
> Strife and war no more she knows,
> Rebel sons nor foreign foes.
> Safe beneath her mighty master
> In security she sits,
> Plants her loose foundations faster,
> And her sorrows past forgets.

And in his *Ode to Peace* in 1718 he continues:

> Thou fairest, sweetest daughter of the skies,
> Indulgent, gentle, life-restoring Peace!
> With what auspicious beauties dost thou rise,
> And Britain's new revolving Janus bless!
> > Awake the golden lyre
> > Ye Heliconian choir!
> > Swell every note still higher,
> > And melody inspire
> > At heaven and earth's desire.
> > Hark, how the sounds agree
> > With due complacency!
> > Sweet Peace! it is all by thee,
> > For thou art harmony.

The hope that the coming peace will bring harmony at
home as well as abroad will be an inspiration in the reconsti-
tuting of industry after the war.   Though difficult, it should
not prove impossible; rather the very difficulty of the task
should be only a spur to our best endeavours.   And so one sees
the possibility of a more contented and harmonious industry,
which may be in itself a portion of the compensation for some
of the sacrifices of the nation.

To sum up, it seems to me that there can be no single forecast of the future of commerce and industry in the first years of the peace. The factors which will determine its state are numerous, and much will depend upon the momentum of each at any given moment. No doubt there will be many surprises, just as there have been during the time of war. But, as regards the general character of trade at that time, these need not be unpleasant ones, provided our expectations are not too great. If the position be faced with courage and tact, it seems that there is little to fear and much to hope. By diverting only a part of the determination, which has been shown on the battlefield, to the arts of peace, very great things can be accomplished. Thus the first need of peace will be to direct the new national spirit to industry and to utilise it to the full. French strategists have a phrase—"the exploiting of a victory"—in the sense of securing the full consequences of a successful operation. The true exploitation of our victory in the world-war will be the securing for the peaceful pursuits of commerce all that is valuable in the lessons which our people have been learning during the time of war.

SAVING AND THE STANDARD
OF LIFE

Τῇ χειρὶ δεῖ σπείρειν, ἀλλὰ μὴ ὅλῳ τῷ θυλάκῳ.

SAVING AND THE STANDARD
OF LIFE

The question of saving received much attention during the greater part of the year 1916, and will become more prominent in the concluding stages of the war. It is, or should be, now unnecessary to add another to the many exhortations which were addressed to the attention of a reluctant public. Rather than this it is proposed to attempt to develop some underlying conditions which appear to me to be fundamental in relation both to the present position and also to that which may be expected to arise in the years of peace. The latter is particularly important in its possible reactions upon the provision of capital for reconstruction to which attention has already been directed.

Theoretically, the Government of a country, which is engaged in a war which is vital to its national existence, has the right of demanding the service of all its subjects and of requisitioning all their wealth. But in regard to the latter there are certain practical difficulties to the obtaining of the whole earnings and liquid wealth of all the people. Naturally the civil population must be allowed to subsist, and the sum for subsistence would vary according to the size of the family. Also it would be in the interest of the State that the efficiency of all kinds of workers should be at least maintained and, if possible, even increased, but the amount necessary for efficiency would vary according to the class of work to be done. Again, there are sums available for the service of the State which could never be obtained by the tax-gatherer, but which will be lent to the Government voluntarily upon a sufficient inducement being offered. Thus the abstract theoretical position encounters the practical administrative difficulty, namely that the State requires immense resources to be obtained rapidly and with the least possible diversion of workers from more urgent kinds of national service to act as revenue officials. Accordingly, a method has been adopted which aims at obtaining a large amount by taxation and the remainder by loan.

During a great war the importance of adequate financial resources cannot possibly be overestimated. Where, as in the case of the Grand Alliance, many nations are fighting together, the resources of which in wealth differ widely, a decisive success will be largely conditioned by the richer nations in the combination being able to supply the needs of those countries whose resources are less developed. The keeping open of trade-routes has enabled the Allies to employ the labour of a very great part of the neutral world in manufacturing for them. But this has involved the payment of the foreign producers, and that again demands that the British Government should have adequate supplies for this and other purposes.

The mechanism of war finance is intricate, but its broader aspects can be easily grasped—if only one starts with the right point of view. The national income has been estimated by some statisticians as exceeding £3,000 millions per annum in 1916. Owing to the rapid rise in prices this figure is uncertain; but, even if it be accepted as a convenient round number, it has to be remembered that war expenditure in 1916–17 exceeded £2,000 millions. With the tendency towards rising prices, it would not be possible to maintain the population upon the balance of the aggregate income if all war-expenditure had been taken by way of tax and loan; and accordingly it has been necessary to draw upon our accumulated wealth by the sale of investments to foreign countries. But there can be little doubt that too great an amount of these has been disposed of, owing to too little having been provided by way of tax and loan, particularly by the former. Foreign investments have been valuable in the past in aiding us in paying for our imports, and in placing us in the position of exporting such goods as we produced at a great relative advantage. If we sell too many of our foreign investments in order to finance the war, we are in danger of being left at a considerable disadvantage in the early years of peace in being compelled to produce exports in order to pay for our imports, which exports may be produced under much less favourable conditions of comparative cost. The fact that much of our present war-expenditure consists of disbursements upon behalf of the Dominions and Allies, for which we shall receive securities later, affords some measure of the extent to which we can afford to sell foreign investments. If those sales do not exceed the amount lent to the Dominions and Allies, the transaction becomes in effect an exchange of external investments, and to that extent, within certain narrow limits, we shall eventually be no better or no worse off. But, if, on the other hand, such sales exceed the sums lent, then *pro tanto* our position after the war would suffer. And to the degree that this exists, saving has proved deficient; while, if saving had been sufficiently great to leave us a surplus upon what has been described as the exchange of foreign investments, to that extent the arrest of our progress in overseas trade during the war, which may show itself in the first years of peace, would be proportionately counteracted.

Moreover the situation must be considered in relation to the demand for commodities. The existence of the huge governmental demand (which is represented quantitatively by the immense war-expenditure) is in effect the call for goods and services which are required for the efficient prosecution of war. To a large extent this is a new demand. Therefore it is necessary that the command over goods and services, which is represented by income, should be diverted from personal expenditure and transferred to the State. Any civilian demand that is in excess of that required for efficiency is, in effect, the employment of labour for non-essential ends,—and, what is more important, the diversion of commodities and services from the forces to purposes which are useless from the standpoint of the national interest. In view of the necessity of the times, it follows that, if the patriotism of the country does not suffice to effect the necessary diversion voluntarily, it must be made compulsorily, more especially since, in the later stages of the war, the supply both of labour and commodities will not suffice for any non-essential consumption.

The movement towards a great increase in saving has been weakened and distracted by much suppressed recrimination between different classes of the community. Each section of the people sees with lynx-eyed clearness the real or alleged extravagances of another section, while it ignores its own. Neither knows nor cares to know of any new sacrifices the other may have made. What is required is a uniform standard, and then for each person to forget that "after-you" attitude of politeness as regards war-savings, and perform his own part. The standard which the times demand is not difficult to define, however hard it may be to attain it in practice. Like other luxuries, that of idle able-bodied workers of any class must be dispensed with, and a war of the magnitude of this one requires the co-operated efforts of all, whether the work be paid or unpaid. In any estimate of the national strength voluntary labour, whether in the care of the wounded or in other directions which increase the efficiency of the forces, must be included; indeed in the past, and never more than in the present, such public service has been one of the glories of the country. For these and other workers of all kinds the standard of expenditure which the circumstances ordain is that which will maintain their respective efficiencies in the duties they are called upon to perform, while all the remainder should be handed over to the State, either in taxation or as a loan. Even if efficiency be interpreted in no narrow sense (since, in order to obtain the best results in invention and ideas, a liberal expenditure upon the worker is necessary) this may seem a hard saying, but in reality it is the course which prudence requires. That a decisive and early victory shall be obtained it is wisest to mobilise our resources for a war of indefinite duration. The Germans and even some of our own unimaginative pessimists have anticipated an early exhaustion of our resources—the former with glee and the latter with a sinking heart. From the beginning of the war I have never doubted that we could

furnish the necessary supplies (provided these are admini-
stered with reasonable economy), not only to the longest date
to which the war could possibly be protracted but even beyond
that date.   Statistics show that this *can* be done and to doubt
that it *will* be done is to assume that the country values money
more than life, that men will risk their lives in battle but that
they will not draw upon their bank balances.   The fact of our
financial endurance may be enough from the financial point
of view, but it is not enough from that of wider national interests.   If we so organise ourselves now that it will prove
beyond the possibility of doubt that we possess the most ample
financial staying power, this will show the enemy that there is
no reasonable chance of his being aided towards a decision by
our financial exhaustion;   and thus peace will be brought
nearer, in part by the adequacy of the supplies so placed at
the disposal of the Grand Alliance, in part by the frustration
of the hopes of their enemies.

A comparison of the demands of the situation with the
actual amount of saving may at first occasion a feeling of keen
disappointment in the mind of the superficial observer.   The
need for conserving our resources for purposes of the war was
only recognised slowly and partially.   But we have to take
our people as we find them, and few of their friends could claim
for them that they are exceptionally gifted with imagination.
Indeed their general attitude in this respect has been a strong
proof of their pacific character, and a pathetic instance to
devotion to the old ways of peace.   At the beginning of the
war it seemed that the peaceful progress of the Victorian era
had been dissolved in the battle chaos of Armageddon, and it
was little wonder that men and women clung to the ideal of the
ordered English home as a small oasis of peace in a world at war.

It would not be just to charge the nation during the early
months of the war with a neglect of its duty and interest.   We
can see now that the Press and responsible public men were
too optimistic.   There appears to have been a most ill-judged
economy of truth when it was feared it would be unpalatable
to the general public.   War upon the present scale was a

wholly new experience, and our rulers seem to have misjudged the fortitude of the people. Therefore the historian of the finance of the Great War will be well advised to estimate the financial sacrifices of the nation in 1914 and 1915, not in the light of his own knowledge of the naval and military situation, but in that afforded by the information then available. More- over, the whole drift of the opinion which had been formed upon the basis of these data was in favour of an early peace, and the expenditure was slow in working towards its maximum. Thus all the popular indications failed to emphasize the great need, even then, for the beginning of rigorous personal economy. Every week during which the public was lulled in a false financial security was creating new difficulties for the future; since, before long, profits and wages in war-industries began to in- crease, and those who received them soon entered upon enlarged scales of expenditure, thus diverting labour from war needs to the production of things which were not necessary.

It is true that the teaching of history should have warned us that the war must involve a tremendous financial strain, and that it was neglecting one of our great assets not to adjust personal expenditures so as to leave a surplus available towards meeting it as soon as possible. But few find in the past any guidance for the present, nor were there any to listen to the warnings of those who pointed out that unproductive consump- tion of wealth in war foreshadowed scarcity in the future.

For these and other reasons the universal national saving which was needed was slow in starting; and, even at the end of 1916, there were many whose income afforded them a surplus beyond the amount required to maintain their efficiency who had not even begun to save. Still, when one considers the whole situation and while it must be admitted that amongst very large sections of the population saving was very far from being upon an adequate scale, there is this to be said in explana- tion, namely that economy to the extent required would involve something of a revolution in accepted standards of living. For many years past the tendency had been towards raising the standard, and this was a slow process. It was one in which the community, in the shape of a certain class or a certain street in a suburb, acted upon the individual, and the individual in his turn reacted upon the community, but both influences had been towards an ascending scale growing gradually by successive accretions. Thus the desires which were satisfied in the spending of income had become welded together in a system in what may be described as superimposed strata of which the lower were regarded as relatively solid and fixed. The marginal calculus was applied rather to the upper strata, usually in the choice amongst alternative additions to the previous desires, sometimes in the substitution of a new satisfaction for a previous one which for some reason was abandoned. It follows that the quantity of saving which is requisite under war conditions introduced a new factor which involved a revision of the whole system of expenditure. The would-be saver would have required to dig down to strata of his desires which he had accepted for long as a fixed part of his life and select some of these which could no longer be satisfied. Further, in the economic life, habit effects a species of incrustation of desire. We have found by sad experience how often the hopes which we cherish in making our purchases deceive us, and the gratification of a new desire is more or less on its trial. We watch it and weigh the result against the expenditure which the gratification of the desire has involved; and if it passes this test, it comes in time to be taken more and more upon trust; and when the habit is once well established, unless there is a considerable alteration in the amount of the income, this desire is not scrutinised in the estimation of the utilities from our purchases. In this way habit becomes a kind of mental, labour-saving device.

The progress of economy will have the effect of breaking through the incrustation of former habits of comparatively free spending; and, in time, new habits will be formed which will be based upon a more Spartan regime of life. Pre-war systems of desires were first broken up, and then gradually re-organised. The desire for national security had been satisfied before the war at a comparatively low cost and that too almost unconsciously, since most of the expenditure upon it was taken from individuals by means of taxation which later experience has shown to have been upon a moderate scale. The war has transformed this desire from being unimportant to one of the greatest moment ; and, instead of being only dimly recognised, it has now come most insistently into consciousness. The duty of the citizen is no longer discharged by providing his quota of taxation, but the needs of the time compel him to give his personal service, and in cases where there is a surplus of income after satisfying his immediate necessities to lend liberally to the State. It follows that a radical change—almost a revolution —has been effected in the system of desires. First the income will frequently be reduced by increased taxation. War prices alone would involve very considerable readjustments in the satisfaction of necessary wants. Scarcity of commodities in the later stages of the war, added to a high level of taxation, will force economy. Some things cannot be purchased, while the consumer of others is rationed. Thus old standards of living are no longer possible. The systems of desires have been broken up, and they will only gradually reconstruct themselves upon a new and lower standard. In fact the concomitants of war have acted as a solvent of habits of expenditure for the majority of the nation in a manner which has not been known for centuries.

This is the inevitable necessity of the psychology of war finance. But a revolution in the systems of desire of a whole nation cannot fail to have noteworthy effects in the future. Voluntarily or involuntarily the war is forcing the formation of habits of economy. From the financial standpoint there is little difference how the result is reached, so long as the resources which are required are in fact obtained ; but from that of the future of commerce and industry the method of economy is of surpassing importance. The conserving of national strength by saving is a conception which does not appeal to the minds of those who have either been brought up in a contempt of niggardliness or who have been nourished on vague but bitter hostility to the abstraction which they term "Capitalism." Upon such weaker brethren economy has to be enforced either by governmental control of certain commodities, or by prohibition of them or by high taxation of luxuries which in extreme cases may become penal. We have no experience of the manner in which the involuntary economy, which measures of this type will enforce, will eventually react upon the standard of life. All that is possible is to reason as to the probable effect from general principles. The first and natural conclusion would no doubt be that the removal of forced economy will promote a reaction and that, when restraint upon purchases of commodities is removed, the tendency will be for the great mass of the public to indemnify themselves for their previous enforced abstinence by making very much larger, if not excessive, purchases. But there are other factors which, though involving several uncertainties at present, tend to limit, if not to counteract, this forecast. It assumes that the system of desires after the war will remain the same as that before it. This is improbable. In the household expenditure of all classes, save the very poorest, there was great waste. The period of scarcity will constitute a time of compulsory training in domestic economy; and, for a time, the fruits of this hard teaching in the school of experience will remain. Then again the standard of life for each class must inevitably be changed, and just as it established itself upon a lower scale with painful slowness, so, when the pressing need for war economy is over, it will move in the reverse direction with considerable deliberateness. Standards of life possess a remarkable inertia and seem incapable of rapid change. Also, if the period of economy is moderately protracted, the force of the formation of new habits must be allowed for. It was this characteristic which delayed the fruits of war saving; but once the dead weight of habit has been overcome, new habits begin to form in a regime of economy, and these again, once they have become established, tend to persist. For these reasons, it may be inferred that even involuntary economy will have some degree of persistence. Nor is this result in any degree vitiated by the commonly expressed consolation that sacrifices of the kind described are only "for the duration of the war." This is one of those devices by which human nature solaces itself when forced to make an abrupt transition which as a rule it detests. There is always a revulsion from the unknown, but when the unknown has become not merely the known but the usual, there is the same disinclination towards change in personal habits. The economies which people first loathed are found after a time to become less distasteful and later they have become entwined with the accepted environment, eventually forming a recognised part of it.

Where economy is voluntary the case is clearer. In many classes much of the pre-war expenditure was not willed explicitly. It was rather ordained by the conventional standard of life of that class. Not infrequently the war has revealed that these standards were wasteful in themselves and that the satisfactions they yielded were vastly overrated. Often they were accepted because people had nothing with which to compare them. Now the opportunity has arisen to contrast the old standard with a new and modified one; and, in terms of utility, the comparison has not been found to favour the former. The growth of indolence and the pursuit of enjoyment in recent years have had the effect of causing the neglect of many of the old household economies. It is still not uncommon to see elderly people who in their youth were the younger members of families which had been brought up during the "hungry forties" exercising numerous small economies, such as the making of paper spills to save matches. The continuance of these practices through two whole generations shows the remarkable persistence of habit. In addition to this influence, there are others which will operate in the same direction. During the war the mutability of human affairs has been dramatically impressed upon everyone. But, fortunately for us, the increased uncertainty has never been so extreme that it has given grounds for anyone to believe that the Fates were implacably hostile to him. Thus it may be expected that there will be a greater disposition to effect savings in order to provide against the future. Many of the conventions which we inherited from the nineteenth century have been dissolved in the smoke of war, and it may be anticipated that some of them will return no more. To some extent the new world of the first years of peace will be full of surprises and risks, for which it is prudent to provide. And to do this will involve the continuance of the saving habits of the war for a number of years after it is ended.

These various lines of thought suggest the general conclusion that a proportion of specific war saving will continue for some years after peace. If this conclusion be well founded, it affords very considerable help towards the solution of a difficult problem which is otherwise perplexing. It appears that the need for capital, when peace has been made, will be exceedingly great. Modern military operations result in a wholesale destruction of buildings and plant in many regions where serious operations have taken place. In addition, the detestable German method of laying waste the towns, villages and even the orchards from which they have been compelled to retreat will involve a very great outlay of capital in restoration. Shipping has suffered, not only by the sinking of vessels by submarines, but also through the arduous nature of the service required from such craft as have been used as auxiliaries to the fleet or as transports. Repairs and extensions of buildings and plant have been postponed in many cases. Such new savings, as have been made by belligerent nations during the war, were employed in aiding the financing of their great war-expenditure, and thus none of them has been able to provide capital (as several of them had been in the habit of doing in the past) for the development of new countries which have hitherto been dependent upon nations with great stores of accumulated wealth for the provision of the larger and more costly improvements, such as railways, harbour facilities and machinery. Hence these new countries have been compelled to postpone many plans for proposed works which had been approved before the war. Thus, if capital is left free to seek its best market after the peace, these countries will compete keenly for it with the home demand for the prosecution of delayed repairs, and both of these again with what will be an even more urgent need, namely the restoration of the material destruction of war in the restoring of ruined buildings, the replacing of injured plant and the construction of new shipping to make good the loss of that which has been sunk.   It is clear that the proportion of the National Dividend saved before the war in Great Britain would be far from sufficient to meet the claims upon it, more particularly when it is remembered that, unless the desire for accumulation is increased, the higher scale of taxation after the war (which will be necessary to pay interest upon the immense war debt) would tend to diminish the surplus from which savings would be made.   Here then we are face to face with one of the vital factors which will aid in determining the rate at which the material losses of the war will be repaired.   And delay tends to be cumulative in its prejudicial effects; since an improvement, postponed through scarcity of capital, bars the way to other subsequent developments which depend upon it.   In fact, in this respect, the war has had the effect of intensifying conditions which had already begun to show themselves.   For the decade prior to the war capital was becoming less abundant.   For this there were two main reasons.   After a long period during which there had been no expensive wars, there came within a short space the Chino-Japanese, the Italo-Abyssinian, the Graeco-Turkish, the Russo-Japanese, the South African and both the Balkan wars. Within this period also rapid progress was being made in the construction of large works and factories in a number of countries which were far from being in a position to supply their own needs for capital.   Hence it is not difficult to imagine the reasons which have led many observers to predict a famine of capital when the great new demands for it are superimposed upon those which existed in 1914.   But reflection should convince us that famine is too strong a word to employ to describe the situation which may be expected to arise.   To some extent the war generated compensations for its own destruction.   Some of the expenditure has gone to provide new factories and plant to increase the output of munitions and other supplies.   In so far as these instruments of production can be adapted to the making of commodities which are in demand in time of peace, to that extent the return of peace will find a number of industries both more fully and more adequately equipped than they were prior to the war. It is true that the distribution of capital in industry during the war has been imperfect when considered in relation to the requirements of peace. From that point of view some industries will have too much capital in fixed plant and buildings, and others will have too little. Then in another direction war-expenditure has not been all loss. Neutrals who have been supplying belligerents with food, munitions and other supplies have increased their trade, and they have been adding to their capital at an increased rate during the progress of hostilities. Hence it follows that one or two which were already lending nations in 1913 will be able to add to their annual exports of capital, if they desire to do so. Others, which had been formerly borrowing nations, will be in a position to supply a larger proportion of their future needs for capital, but it is probable that not many will be transferred from the class of debtor, to that of creditor, countries.

When all is said it remains true that, if these grounds only be taken into consideration, capital would be exceedingly scarce. Granting that neutrals will be so situated that they will have more to invest and that the war itself will have over-capitalised a few industries, there remain all the needs of making good war's destruction and postponed improvements in the belligerent countries and of meeting the balance of the demand of new countries. It is in this connection that several of the British Dominions are in danger of being great sufferers. Their exceedingly patriotic contributions of men and money have placed them at a serious disadvantage as contrasted with neutral nations which were in an approximately similar stage of economic development. Therefore, unless the Dominions can obtain capital to overtake a part of the arrears of development they are liable to find their progress arrested and their relative position as producers to have deteriorated as compared with the Argentine. But it is fortunate that there is a way of escape from this suggestion, not indeed of stagnation but of seriously arrested growth. There remains the possibility of increased saving being continued for a considerable period after the end of the war. " For the duration of the war " was accepted as a species of Abracadabra which postponed, if it did not solve, all our most pressing difficulties. But no economic difficulty can be placed in cold storage, in the sense that it remains fixed and immobile till it is brought back to the outer air. The insistent call made by the needs of mankind always causes efforts to be put forth to satisfy them, and, if one type of want is suppressed (though this is often difficult), other new wants arise to take its place. Thus when the factors, which had been withdrawn, are restored to the world of industry, it is found to be changed. It follows that there will be few cases in which economic conditions have been postponed for the period of the war where they can be restored in their former environment; while they have been held in abeyance, their former environment has been changing. In the special case of accumulation, war saving has been slowly forcing a revision of standards of life, and experience begins to show that this fundamental revision has revealed prospects of a less complex scale of living. Moreover the formation of new habits of saving, once they are well established, will have a tendency to persist. The inertia of social customs is both exceedingly great and protracted. The driving force of the necessities of war was at first—at least in appearance—broken against this powerful resistance. But as the war progressed, gradually, though with painful slowness and with exasperating deliberateness, the mass of habit and custom began slowly to change, and that change itself will become fixed with a marked tendency to persist. J. S. Mill speaks of the phenomenon which I have been describing as an authentic and highly important psychological fact when actions, "which men originally did for a motive of some sort, they continue to do from habit. Sometimes this is done unconsciously, the consciousness coming only after the action: at other times with conscious volition, but volition which has become habitual and is put into action by the force of habit, in opposition perhaps to the deliberate preference." Therefore it follows that the economy of war time will become largely habitual; and, even though it was begun for a special object with a definite time limit, after the end of the war it may be expected that, for these reasons, saving will be considerably larger than it was immediately before the war. This conclusion affords very considerable prospects of an augmentation of the quantity of capital which will be necessary to diminish the industrial and social stagnation which would otherwise have been caused by hostilities. Adequate capital will be the cordial which will best revive commerce when it can flourish again in a peaceful world. This prospect holds out hope for the future and a definite exhortation for the immediate present. Saving during war time is trebly advantageous. It possesses the usual benefit of constituting a provision for the saver, it is incumbent upon non-combatants as their aid towards the prosecution of the war and finally, in the manner which I have shown, it will be a material aid in the reconstitution of industry when peace returns.

ORGANISATION RE-ORIENTATED

Οἷόν ἐστιν ἐν ἡνωμένοις τὰ μέλη τοῦ σώματος, τοῦτον ἔχει τὸν λόγον ἐν διεστῶσι τὰ λογικὰ, πρὸς μίαν τινὰ συνεργίαν κατεσκευασμένα.

MARCUS AURELIUS.

ORGANISATION RE-ORIENTATED

It has been said that the examination which was held formerly for candidates who desired to enter the service of the Chinese Government was the most exhaustive test of the kind in the world. But there is another unperceived examination which is even more thorough. That is the criticism to which our theories will be submitted by posterity. Just as we, in our turn, signalise the shortcomings of our predecessors and sometimes wonder at the conclusions which seemed to stare them in the face but which somehow or other they failed to apprehend; so, in the future, our own analyses and the interpretations of the things we experience will be examined similarly —and doubtless with a precisely similar result. That clarity of vision, which the lapse of time gives to most intellectual processes, will have been at work, revealing defects of investigation and weaknesses in reasoning. Moreover, the simile of an examination suggests an interesting speculation in the treatment of the economic enquiries of a past generation by that which succeeds it. To some extent the examiners cannot be fully equipped for their task, for they can never have a first-hand acquaintance with the phenomena, concerning the interpretation of which they must act as judges. It is necessary for them to pronounce an opinion mainly from an analysis of what has been written by their predecessors, interpreted by the commentary which has been furnished by the progress of events. But the written word is very far from being adequate as the vehicle by which economic meanings are to be expressed. The investigator always sees more in the phenomena than he actually records in what he is able to write about them; and, not only so, but the meaning his words convey to him will be slightly different from that gathered from them by his readers. Also, a striking analysis or an attractive theory soon becomes stereotyped in a term or a phrase; and this natural labour-saving device for the mind usually means a loss of meaning. The naming of theories, almost invariably, involves a sacrifice of the full reality of thought. This is a common experience in many studies. The foundation of a school, too, often means the gradual sterilising of the richness and completeness of the attitude of mind which initiated the new development. What was at first a living thought becomes conventionalised, and may at last end by being no more than a phrase. And economic studies seem to be peculiarly subject to this defect. The material with which they deal is continually changing, at least in its external form and sometimes, it may be, in many of its more essential characteristics. Thus renewed efforts must be made to reduce to scientific rule its somewhat Protean variations; and, once the first path has been beaten out, each succeeding wayfarer wears something away from it. It is true that a few may add much, they may cut off an occasional corner or smooth down an approach which was at first too steep for comfort and convenience. But the fact seems to remain that the words, which enable the truth to be revealed, at the same time almost might be imagined to be jealous of that revelation, and they in time come to imprison a part of the original living thought which they were designed to perpetuate. And, further, a terminology eventually becomes a species of *idola fori*. As it grows popular, it acquires a species of momentum. It is like a moving stairway upon which one steps without being conscious of its existence and which carries us on when in fact we imagine we are standing still.

It is needless to say that classification, definitions and terminologies are necessary and are exceedingly helpful. But it is advisable, at the same time, to recognise that they have certain minor disadvantages, and a clear statement of these will go some way towards the neutralising of them. To overcome them completely is not possible—that can only be accomplished when, in the fullness of time, there has been a sufficient interval to provide a verification of the theory or upon the contrary to produce the phenomena which show that the theory was incomplete.

These general reflections are suggested by what one may imagine those subsequent generations, which will examine our work, may say of it. In a dim way, which may be the fore-runner of a new dawn or which again may itself be only a "false dawn," one feels that perhaps in a few directions the economics of the present day may suffer some degree of danger through having being captured by phrases—which are good servants but the worst possible masters. They are like the old family retainer—who is more often met with in fiction than in real life. He makes himself indispensable and one comes to depend upon him more and more, till in the end he dictates rather than serves. In something the same way the word or the phrase, which was once the epitome of an analysis of a group of phenomena, comes to be taken as a formula, and then as a substitute for enquiry. Thus there is the danger of what metaphysicians call the hypostatisation of an abstraction. Further it may happen that the word or phrase which at the beginning was no more than the condensed expression of analysis may come in time to gather to itself accretions of meaning, which involve theory as well as analysis. And the difficulty becomes intensified if, by frequent use, the fine edges of the original meaning will be, as it were, worn away, and the accre-tions of signification differ in different minds, though the precise divergencies may not be formulated.

It may be wondered if some process of the kind described may not have begun to happen in connection with the term "organisation." It would be difficult to discover a recent systematic treatise on the theory of Political Economy which does not mention the "organisation of industry," and since the beginning of the war, we have heard much of organisation in very many connections and the term is used once more to indicate anticipated or desired changes in industry when the war will have been ended.

All students of economics will have a conception of what

is meant by the organisation of industry. This description replaced the older one of "division of labour" and that of still earlier date, namely "system"—though the latter survives in the common title of "a system of Political Economy." The meanings derived from the source whence organisation itself comes have themselves varied. Aristotle meant something very different from what the modern reader might have expected, when he called his Logic, τὸ Ὄργανον. "Organon" to the Greek conveyed, as its root significance, the idea of instrument, just as we continue to speak of church organs, the conception being that of *the* musical instrument. Thus the original "organisation" would have been—to make a somewhat unpleasing compound—instrumentalisation, that is to cause anything to serve as an instrument or even as a tool. But, by the time the term was used by economists, the prevalence of the evolutionary doctrine had superadded a distinct meaning, namely the idea of something living, as when we speak of an organism or of organic; and it was in this sense that the adoption of organisation by economists was in effect the announcement of a new truth or at least a new point of view, namely the characterisation of specialised industry working for a common end as a special kind of social organism, and it has always seemed to me that the organisation of industry was precisely that process by which such an individual organism came into existence.

At this point, analysis, almost unconsciously, becomes involved in theory. In a sense an industrial organism is a metaphor. It resembles the earlier distinction between natural and artificial bodies, as when "the body politic" was included under the latter heading. The social organism is in reality no more than an analogical expression, and there is no little danger of confusion if we treat it in reasoning as anything more than the intellectual counter which in fact it is. No doubt we can speak of an industrial organism "adapting itself to its environment," of its "developing new functions," of "its possession of rudimentary organs," of its "struggle for existence," and so on. But after all, these expressions are similitudes, not the actual descriptions of the real process. The close contact of Economics with other sciences has often led it to borrow much from them, not only in positive data but in the more subtle way of adopting their point of view. In this case the economist has learnt the language of the evolutionary biologist; and, in using that language, he is influenced by its theoretical implications. These, from their nature, are adapted to describing the physical rather than the human and mental relationship, and the tendency is to regard industrial processes perhaps a little too much from the outside. We reach an admirable life-history of industrial organisms, but we may not have yet penetrated to the full comprehension of their inner consciousness, simply because the apparatus of investigation does not include the necessary equipment. When we endeavour to conceive an industrial organism in its inner meaning, it will be found to contain within itself the idea of its own development. It not only adapts itself to its environment but, even more, it adapts that environment to itself. Accordingly, adaptation involves not so much the fitting of the organism to something external to itself, but *to its own self externalised*, that is to say, it may modify a previous environment, and the new environment will thus contain the effect of that action. It will no longer be wholly alien, but will include in it the working of the organism, but separated off from itself. Later that organism may feel a need to adjust itself to its surroundings as now constituted; but, in so acting, it is in reality fitting itself to external things which are not wholly alien, but embody in them a former activity of the organism.

The industrial organisation, with which the economist is concerned, involves an organiser or organisers whose function it is to provide the plan or scheme and also to see that it works. Into that plan there must be fitted both animate and conscious agents and inanimate things. Either class may be tractable or intractable. They may co-operate in the general plan or they may enter into it only under constraint. The Physiocrats were in the habit of speaking of Nature working with man, but Nature at that time was rather personified. The truth seems to be that inanimate forces and things sometimes lend themselves to an industrial scheme and sometimes they do not; and, in the latter case, they are only made tractable with great difficulty. As a mere speculation the difference in their behaviour might be explained by a theory of monads of varying degrees of affinity to man, or in other ways. In principle, the co-operation of the human agents in a scheme of production should be harmonious, if we postulate that each is free to enter upon it or not, as he pleases. If, on the other hand, they are assigned to their work by forces outside their own control, they may be expected to resist, since their labour will tend to become in essence forced labour. Their freedom as human beings has been taken from them and, unless they sink to a merely sentient existence, they will strive to assert it, even if only by chafing against the bonds which they feel are confining them. It is only possible that this resistance should be avoided, if all were satisfied with the wisdom and beneficence of the power which assigned them to the special task which they were called upon to perform. In the actual world of to-day neither of the two conditions, just described, is fulfilled exactly. The great majority of people are certainly not assigned a definite task upon rigorous conditions as to the kind of work and the place where it is to be carried on. But, on the other side, freedom is not perfect. It is limited in many directions, sometimes by want of early opportunities, sometimes by the choice made once for all by parents. Hence it often happens that the subordinate human elements in the carrying out of a scheme of production only co-operate imperfectly. The imperfection of this relationship gives rise to another tendency which is exceedingly interesting from this point of view. There is not only organisation of production but also organisation of labour. The fact is plain, but the idea of it is possibly somewhat perplexing from the evolutionary standpoint. We start with the conception of relatively self-complete, so-called, industrial organisms. But one function of these, namely the labour, sets up an independent organisation of its own. In its initial form this was simple and intelligible, where, for instance, the workers in one organism formed an organisation of their own. But under modern conditions we find a great extension, whereby the workers, not only in a whole trade, but also in several trades, form an organisation to protect their interests; while, at the same time, they continue to discharge their original functions in the productive organisation to which they belong. This development constitutes a species of giddy dance of biological categories. Functions split off from the primary organism assume new forms and yet remain in their original *milieu*. And the situation is further complicated by the complementary organisation of yet another set of functions, cutting again across the conception of the productive organism, in so far as employers again organise to resist the pressure of those they employ. When one considers the essentials of the situation it may be conjectured that the conception of industrial organisms seems to be on the way to pass into another which may eventually absorb it. May it not be that there will be a development towards a homogeneous organisation of each factor in production which discharges any relatively distinct function—such for instance, as organisation of enterprising ability, waiting, the bearing of risk and so on? The idea of an extended federation of industries in the same trade and of those in allied trades seems to point in this direction. This would ultimately result, at least in appearance, in a few very large organisations, each fighting for the maintenance of its own function, and that to the apparent detriment of the other functions. The productive organisms would seem to be in process of transformation into distributive organisms. But to continue the biological metaphor, there may not only be an extensive character in organisation, it may become fissiparous; at a certain stage, minor functions may break off from the organisation in which they were formerly contained and form a new one of their own. This would be almost inevitable, for it is difficult to see how these monster organisations could be formed and continue without in the end causing a grave restriction of the freedom of the members. The latter would be in danger of discovering that they had bartered their liberty for what turned out to be no more than a mess of pottage in the scheme of distribution.

Further, unless the nation is to be completely industrialised, the organisations, which have just been discussed, will never contain all the people. Therefore behind them there still remains the State. What is to be its relation to industrial organisation—will the close connection of war-time continue or will there be a reversion to some stage varying between the discontinuity of the middle of the nineteenth century and the somewhat querulous attitude of the first decade of the twentieth? In the first period the State aimed at playing the part of an Epicurean god, in the second at being a human providence—and neither with any great success. Centralisation, under a democratic system, means devolution by successive stages; and war-time experience points to the conclusion that organisation becomes more and more entangled in a labyrinth of committees—the career of which may recall the sharp saying of a writer during the Civil Wars, namely that these bodies are *bona peritura*[1].

Nor are these the only possibilities. It is not only a question of the State controlling industry, but also the converse one of industry or of a group of industries exerting an undue influence upon policy. This seems to be a case in which we have been affected, especially since the war, by German methods. It is now believed that the Prussian bureaucracy was successful in directing commerce towards large national ends. This in effect was the neo-mercantilism which flourished during the years of the spiritual decline of Germany. It may be a good maxim "fas est et ab hoste doceri," but, in this respect, our attitude may be judged to be more than a little illogical, since the fundamental cause of conflict has been the different and irreconcilable ideas of living; and, at the core of the German system, which we repudiate, has been the denial of the British conception of personal freedom through a system of over-elaborated organisation. Granted that we are not a logical race, it would probably surpass even our capacity for digesting contradictions to wage a war at an enormous expenditure of

---

[1] C. Walker, *Relations and Observations*, 1650, p. 14.

life and treasure in order to be free to lead our own lives, and then when the struggle was ended to accept voluntarily a great part of that very conception of living against which we had waged war. To do this would be, in the graphic phrase of an old writer, "to fight our liberty into slavery." It is true that nations have done even stranger things than this, but the example is not one which calls for imitation.

The primary idea of industrial organisation was productive, then it seemed to veer towards a growing emphasis upon distributive conditions and to that it is possible that ends of State-policy may be added. In the biological reference there is implicit something of a teleological reference, and it is not out of place to ask what is the end of industrial elaboration. The simple creed of Adam Smith with its belief in "the invisible hand" solved all difficulties by finding the greatest common good in the free play of that division of labour which we now call organisation. At the moment we think more of the "hidden hand" than of "the invisible hand," showing a shifting of the point of view whence may follow actual action which will have important commercial and social consequences. A very few years ago most economists, if they had been forced somewhat reluctantly to define the end of organisation, would have found it either in the more efficient production, or possibly in the more equitable distribution, of wealth. But, again, there is the sceptical query how far does organisation in its modern developments affect either end in reality? Attention has already been drawn to the segregation of functions which may be conceived to tend towards an internecine struggle. This, however, is not to be taken without further enquiry as an absolutely disadvantageous state. There are some forms of activity which only reach their maximum effects when they encounter resistance. Accordingly, it may at least be imagined that industrial activity is of such a nature that internal friction, or even strife, is conducive to progress instead of being a restraint upon progress. No doubt to the manager who is fresh from a fruitless discussion with the representative of a Trade Union or to the Labour leader who has recently met an intractable employer this may appear a far-fetched and baseless abstraction. Each conscious agent who takes part in the carrying out of a scheme of production is apt to consider his function as being the whole or representative of the whole of the process. But when that process is considered in its entirety and each function is relegated to its proper place, it is at least conceivable that a moderate amount of internal friction is stimulative in the end. While that view is maintainable, there are reasons against its final acceptance. Assuming even that a moderate amount of resistance is required to call forth the best activity, that is likely to be found, during as long a period as one need consider, in the resistance which some of the forces of Nature will continue to offer to being harnessed to the service of man. The added resistance, arising from defective co-operation and often positive hostility amongst the human factors, represents an unnecessary hindrance which, as it seems to me, must inevitably hinder progress, whether it be conceived over a moderately long period or over a very long one. This is clear as regards the former, but not perhaps altogether as regards the latter. Might it not be argued that, as functions become effete, a certain amount of internal disturbance is required to free the industrial organism of them? It is true that external conditions would serve the same end eventually. Competition means the removal of dying or dead methods. But competition may be conceived as exerting its full force in the world of atomic, industrial organisms, where each was relatively free to survive or perish as the fates, as evolution, ordained. But if the possible trend of organisation, not according to firms but according to industrial functions, be a possibility, it is obvious that competition will be limited. The scale upon which it operates will be immensely enlarged, but its working will be slow and much less flexible. It would produce not changes but revolutions. Under these circumstances new adjustments in these few large organisms should come by mutual internal adaptations from within, effected not by violence, but by co-operation.

Then there is the other alternative already outlined, namely that these overgrown organisations will be themselves unstable.

Should they succeed in establishing themselves, their very magnitude may bear within it the seeds of dissolution. Megalomania appears to have extended from the dream of power and wealth to that of social arrangements. It may well be questioned whether it can develop in such a manner as to include efficiently within it the diversified temperaments and abilities of a people with racial individuality, which again is the germ of initiative. Standardised humanity, which has been the dream of some social idealists, is not only a delusion; but, if it were possible in this country, it would be that evil form of slavery which conquers the mind by a subtle education begun from the earliest years when the victims—for victims they would be—were unable to resist.

So far the biological conception of evolution may lead us, but beyond the result becomes an *impasse*. It may be that at present this is as far as the available information, even when helped liberally by speculation, can extend. But it is at least worth attempting an envisaging of the situation apart from some entangling implications in the terminology we have been using. It appears that there are two fundamental facts in the situation. One is the framing and working out of a plan which requires to use both human and natural agents. The other is that the human co-operation is not wholly voluntary; and groups of these agents, while continuing to perform their task in the scheme of production, unite with others, whose interests are similar, and this association may impede the execution of the original plan of production—as for instance in the case of a strike or lock-out. In fact there are two different kinds of relations belonging to the same people and which may be antagonistic, as in the case of Syndicalism. As already hinted, this cutting across lines of economic division may increase further with new kinds of association. And, if the State becomes directly involved, the centre of gravity suffers a radical change. The citizen cannot be dissociated from his economic activities, and still less the economic activities from the citizen. The human industrial unit is held to need the care of the State in some of his industrial relations, as in the case of the Factory Acts or of Labour Exchanges. During the war experience has shown that all the belligerent States have exerted very large measures of control over industry, commerce and credit. No doubt there have been special reasons which have made this course inevitable or appear to have been inevitable. It is a usual experience that Governments are slow to relinquish authority which they have assumed even temporarily. And what complicates the future position is that this relationship of the State to commerce has at least two sides. On one of these, new limits to individual initiative are imposed. The State lays down new conditions which must be taken into account in the framing of industrial plans. But on the other hand, the intervention of the State is believed by many to introduce helps rather than hindrances. There are industries to which its active intervention will bring some advantage. Thus a closer relation of the State to trade would introduce another line of cleavage in industrial association. First it would divide all those interests which believed that they secured advantage by aid from the State in any form from all the remaining interests. But it might be expected that some of the trades and other bodies which thought they would secure benefit from such intervention would find by experience that they procured either only an inconsiderable one or possibly a balance of disadvantage. Hence the non-advantaged interests would be reinforced as time went on. Eventually, though not immediately, a reaction might be expected; and, after the tide of State-action in relation to industry had flowed strongly, it would later begin to ebb. It would follow that in time, though possibly after a considerable time, State-action would diminish. Too much should not be made of the control of industry during the war, because when the circumstances are examined closely, it may fairly be contended that it is not so much the State that has taken over certain industries, as that certain functions of the great public departments have been delegated to representatives of these industries, under certain broad principles mutually agreed upon. It is too soon yet to pronounce upon the consequences, both direct and indirect, but there are disadvantages which have already begun to reveal themselves for those who are able to look beneath the surface. Further, the special peculiarity of industry during a period of hostilities must be carefully noted. At a vast number of points it must be subservient to efficiency in the waging of war. Some trades supply the forces, others have to be limited because their ramifications are dangerous, others are checked by a withdrawal of labour to augment the army or by a reduction of raw materials in the interests of national endurance, others again must be encouraged as a means of aiding in the rectifying of the Exchanges. It would seem that all this would pass away soon after the declaration of peace. But that may or may not happen according to circumstances. If it be the general desire to re-establish civil life as soon as possible and as quickly as possible, all the interferences of the State with trade (which have just been described) ought to be abandoned, not indeed suddenly, but with the least delay which is compatible with as easy a transition as can be effected from war-conditions to peace-conditions. That is one alternative, but there is another. It may be that feelings of hostility against the late enemies will outlast actual war, and at the moment this appears to be not improbable. In that case, commerce will continue to retain some of its war-time organisation. It will be militant not missionary; and, to that extent, it will be directed by political and not by strictly economic aims. It follows necessarily that in these activities it would be in close relationship with the State.

In the minds of many this whole question is represented exclusively as one of tariffs. But it is vastly greater than that. The regulation of foreign commerce by means of customs duties is only one aspect—and that not the most important— of the action of the State with regard to commerce. What really is most important is the mental attitude. The former one was individualistic, in so far as each distinct industrial entity endeavoured to do the best it could for itself by its own powers. If it accepts and relies upon State-assistance it must pay the price in a certain sacrifice of initiative on balance. State-aid to some industries may give scope for larger schemes and for greater projects, but it can only be to the detriment of all the remaining trades in which the tendency will be towards a limitation of enterprise. The fundamental problem will be the extent to which industry will barter its freedom for State-assistance. Curiously enough the answer seems to be determined more by psychological than by purely economic considerations. During the last quarter of a century, in spite of almost endless disappointments, there has been a growing disposition to rely upon the State. This seems to be mainly an attitude of mind. It may be in part a reaction against the extreme and almost anarchical individualism of the third quarter of the nineteenth century. Also the administration of public departments has been greatly improved, and it would be illusory to apply much of what early economists wrote about governmental action to that of the present day. Yet behind all this, one seems to discern traces of a certain national fatigue, which is by no means indisposed to cast some of its burdens from its shoulders on the proverbial broad back of the State. Here, more than ever, one longs for some charm that would wrest the secret which the future holds. Will the new national spirit be more energetic and self-reliant than the old? Will it come with a sense of power, and a desire to be self-sufficient? Or again will it discover some means of uniting the general and the individual interest, without the sacrifice of the freedom and initiative of the latter? The causes which will make the eventful decision are already coming into existence, but as yet it is impossible to detect the character and more particularly the power which each will exert in the final result.

What then is the conclusion to which the various aspects of the previous discussion lead or is any conclusion possible? Although no single precise answer can be given, certain elements of a statement may perhaps be discovered. In the first place the prevalent idea of industrial organisation seems to miss certain parts of the truth through some of the implications of evolutionary theory. Progress is considered rather from the outside, and the form of statement is better adapted to the biological conception of animate but non-intelligent existences, than to that of the effort of man with his consciousness, will and reason. Thus we obtain something of a life-history of the industrial system, but we seem to be in danger of failing to find its soul. We are shown a mere process when in fact, as it seems to me, we are faced with a problem. That problem is not mathematical, physical or biological, but at once intellectual and emotional. From one point of view it embodies the ceaseless striving of man to express himself in the work of his mind or of his hands. If he is organised in the old Greek sense of being a mere instrument, used as a tool by another, then so far his daily toil is something that not only neglects but is even alien to his humanity. Thus there is a lack of harmony in the human factors which co-operate only partially in a scheme of production. The problem of the future will be the harmonising of this discord. Man is on the way to master inanimate things, but hitherto the failure has been in treating human beings too much like things. Man's place in industry is not to be mastered but to provide free and willing service. Specialisation of industry has specialised skill and at the same time it has gone far towards eliminating interest in the actual product of any large scheme of production. In this respect the master-craftsman of the Middle Ages had a marked advantage over the artisan of to-day. The armourer, the mason or the silversmith not only took a pride in his work, but he marked it with his sign. Individuality of skill has been lost in the complexity of mass-production. Thus the problem will be to complete specialisation by giving it a soul. Our industrial organism is as yet barely half alive, to reach its full development it must devise means of securing the harmonious co-operation of the full mental and physical energies of all the specialised human functions in production. As it is Man stands against Nature with the better half of his powers unused, because he is divided against himself.

And so one sees the vision of what the work of the world might be. Industrial production at present has no common mind, only hands. It has yet "to find itself" in the sense of discovering it is not a mere process but something much more than that.

In order to reach its full development, it must succeed in awakening a general consciousness with a common will. Each worker requires to contribute his own special skill and at the same time to recognise it as a part of the whole which he thereby aids in producing. As Man in industry becomes reconciled to himself, it will be possible for him to advance to a degree of control over Nature which will be much greater than that of the present. Thus there is a possibility of external things becoming in some dim future not merely tractable but even malleable to the mind and the will of man.

This, it may be said, is economic Idealism. And one ventures to say why not? Is it not a mean view of economic study to confine it to classifying and analysing phenomena, without endeavouring to see where its generalisations appear to be tending? The physical scientist points out where the things with which his special study is concerned are either not used or not used to the best advantage. May not the economist try to show how in our present system much of human power is simply waste material? According to most of the thinking that has long been prevalent this may seem to be a reversal of the economic point of view and to be almost revolutionary. But if the conclusions be well founded, and if it is recognised that there is a great problem confronting our whole industrial life, we should be more than half-way towards the solution. In few cases is the saying of Hesiod that the beginning is half the whole, more true[1]; and, like other practical problems, the solution may prove easier than the mere recognition that there *was* a problem for which a solution was required. When the time comes and that solution has been discovered, the next generation may recognise it as a new industrial revolution, greater than that of the eighteenth century, for it will transform the relation of men to men not that of men to machines. And perhaps when some economic historian comes to write about it all at a later date, he will often pause to wonder why it was so long before it was noticed that so great a need existed.

[1] Ἀρχὴ ἥμισυ παντός.

APPENDIX

APPENDIX

STATISTICS OF SHIPPING DURING WAR, WITH LOSSES AND THE AMOUNT OF SHIPBUILDING

I. Number of Ships, Great Britain and Colonies, 1792, 1803, 1913.

	Numbers	Tonnage	Average tons per ship
1792	16,079	1,540,145	96
1803	20,893	2,167,863	104

	Numbers	net	gross	Average tons per ship
1913[1]	20,938	12,119,891	19,604,900	932

II. Losses of Shipping, 1803 to 1814[2].

	Tons
Tonnage of Ships, 1803	2,167,863
Ships built, 1803 to 1814[3]	1,089,067
Increase in Prize ships remaining on the Register[4]	205,674
	3,462,604
Tonnage of Ships in 1814	2,616,965
Losses and Deductions 1803–1814[5]	845,639

[1] United Kingdom only.

[2] State Papers, Admiralty Records, Secretary's Department, Misc. 354–357; Treasurer's Ledger, Greenwich Hospital; High Court of Admiralty, Misc. 491, 492; Chalmers, *Comparative Strength of Great Britain*; Colquhoun, *Treatise on Wealth, Power and Resources of the British Empire*; Porter, *Progress of the Nation* (1838); *Hansard*, 1814–1815; Danson, *Our Next War*; Norman, *The Corsairs of France*.

[3] The Records of the Custom House for 1812 and 1813 were destroyed by fire, and the shipbuilding for those years has been taken at the average of 1811 and 1814.

[4] This form of statement (which is the only one possible in the circumstances) underestimates the losses, since prize ships lost, retaken by the French or destroyed are not counted. Also, if there was an excess of ships purchased over ships sold, the amount of that excess would swell the losses.

[5] For the reasons stated in the previous note this figure is to be taken as a minimum one.

III. *Prizes taken from the French and by the French* 1803–1814, *and records of shipbuilding in the United Kingdom and the Colonies.*

	French ships taken by the British	British ships taken by the French	Ships built in Great Britain and in the Colonies	
			Number	Tonnage
1803	33	222	1407	135,692
1804	53	387	991	95,979
1805	39	507	1001	89,584
1806	33	519	772	69,198
1807	33	559	770	68,000
1808	49	469	568	57,140
1809	28	571	596	61,396
1810	67	619	685	84,891
1811	37	470	870	115,638
1812	34	475	867[1]	106,800[1]
1813	18	371	867[1]	106,800[1]
1814	16	145	864	97,949

IV. *Ships prosecuted as Prize from* 1803 *to* 1807.

A little further light upon the shipping position can be obtained from a return to Parliament entitled a "Paper presented to the House of Commons respecting Ships prosecuted as Prize during the late War and the Present[2]." This return only records the name of the vessel and that of its commander. The majority of these were neutrals. There is much duplication. Apparently the same ship reappears several times in the list, and in a number of cases mention is made of a vessel being prosecuted on its second and even its third capture. Some small war-ships are included, and it appears there may have been English craft charged with trading with the enemy[3]. Of the total prosecuted, there are no particulars as to how many were actually condemned as prizes. The following are the totals of the ships prosecuted:

1803	468
1804	289
1805	485
1806	840
1807	869
	2,951

It will be seen from the previous appendix that this total was not greatly in excess of the ships seized and actually condemned by the French in the same period.

---

[1] Estimated. [2] *Accounts and Papers*, 1808, IX. 173.

[3] The *Lord Nelson*, prosecuted in 1807, was likely to have been an English ship.

INDEX

Printed in the United States
By Bookmasters